THE ESSENTIAL
GROWTH
MINDSET
Handbook
for Teens

ISBNs: 9798851742675 (hardcover), 9798851671913 (paperback)

THE ESSENTIAL
GROWTH
MINDSET
Handbook
for Teens

A Comprehensive 50-Day Growth Mindset Program Nurturing Resilience, Confidence and Problem Solving Skills

---

By Richard Meadows

RAISEYOUTHRIGHT

STINK EYE

Preface

Every moment felt like a battle. A constant struggle to prove that I was good enough, smart enough, talented enough. As a teen, my mind was my greatest foe. It was all about performance, about outdoing the rest, about acing every test. And the fear of failing? It haunted my dreams.

Schoolwork, exams (just thinking about them gives me shivers), sports, fitting in... each one was a mountain to conquer. And the struggle was real. It consumed my thoughts, my time, and my energy, leaving little space for the fun and laughter that should have been a part of my teenage years.

One time, I had the opportunity to participate in a major debate competition. Exciting, right? But instead of relishing the experience, I was crippled by fear. The fear of messing up, of stumbling over my words, of letting my team down. It felt like the weight of the world was on my shoulders. And guess what? I messed up. Badly.

But did the world end? Did everyone abandon me? Nope. There were consequences, sure. I was disappointed, my team was disappointed. But we moved on. Life moved on. And the catastrophic event I had dreaded? It wasn't as earth-shattering as I had feared. Looking back, it was a learning experience, one of many that life had in store for me.

I'm sharing this with you because it's a classic example of the pitfalls of a fixed mindset. If we're not careful, it can rob us of the joy, the wonder, and the incredible learning experiences that life has to offer.

If I could whisper some wisdom into the ear of my teenage self, it would be this: embrace the struggle. It's okay to mess up. In fact, it's necessary. It's all part of the journey. And remember, not every stumble is a fall. More often than not, it's a chance to learn, grow, and to become stronger.

If my story resonates with you, know that you're not alone. Teenagers, just like adults, grapple with these challenges. But here's the thing, these years are a time of exploration, discovery, and, yes, growth. While you might feel grown, your mind and your attitudes are still evolving.

Being a teenager is like being on a rollercoaster. There's the thrill of new experiences, the nerve-wracking firsts—first time driving, first time in high school, first dates, maybe a first job. Add to that the pressures of academics, the influence of social media, and the constant need to stay connected... it's a whirlwind! All these experiences are shaping who you are and who you're becoming. But let's face it: it's also pretty overwhelming.

The good news is, there's a way to navigate this exciting yet challenging phase. You can learn to see failures as opportunities, to embrace challenges, to enjoy the process of learning. That's where a growth mindset comes in, and that's what this book is all about.

Who am I?

Hey, it's Richard Meadows here, and I was once the teen who had a near-
 phobia of messing up. I lived with this endless echo in my mind, telling me I needed to be perfect all the time. From acing tests to winning at sports, I felt like I had to excel in everything, no matter what.

My folks were always there for me, rooting for me, but they expected a lot. I desperately wanted to make them beam with pride, but the more I tried, the tougher it seemed. The more I tried to dodge mistakes, the more I tripped. It was like being caught in a loop.

People used to tell me, "keep at it, you'll make it." But the *how* was never answered. How could I keep at it when the very idea of failing had me breaking out in cold sweats? I knew I had to crack this puzzle. I knew I had to break out of this constant fear.

I don't remember the precise moment it clicked for me, but I knew something had to change. The pressure, the self-doubt, the constant dread... it was too much. So, there I was, with a choice to make: would I keep striving for unattainable perfection, scared out of my wits about messing up? Or would I stare down my fear, shift gears, and learn to see my mistakes as growth opportunities?

I chose to shift gears. I decided to seek out a new mindset, a different way to handle challenges. I read heaps of books, attended talks, consulted professionals, and posed question after question. I was driven to understand why I was so scared of failing and how I could flip that fear on its head.

Over time, I uncovered and tested out various strategies that helped me switch from a fixed to a growth mindset. I learned to see failures not as boulders blocking my path, but as stepping stones. And now, I want to share these insights with you.

I believe that no one should live in constant fear of messing up or not measuring up. **I want to help you see that making mistakes is not just okay— it's a crucial part of growth.** This book will have bits that speak to your parents or guardians because they're part of this journey too, but the main aim here is to give you the tools to cultivate a growth mindset.

Why this book, why now?

Let's talk about something seriously cool: your mind. You've probably noticed, it's a pretty complex thing. But guess what? The way you think about your own abilities can make a world of difference. And we've got research to back it up!

Studies conducted by the program for international student assessment suggest a vast majority of students worldwide—2 out of every 3—rock what they call a "growth mindset." This mindset is the belief that you can, indeed, get smarter and improve your abilities. And it doesn't stop at making you feel better about yourself; it's linked to better test scores and a greater sense of well-being. In the U.S., A big 70% of students showed a growth mindset and had scores that were solid 60 points higher in reading than their counterparts with a fixed mindset.

But hold on, there's more! Did you know more girls than boys in 39 countries demonstrated a growth mindset? And this attitude paid off by boosting their academic performance. However, the influence of a growth mindset differs from country to country. In Estonia, for instance, over 75% of students showed a growth mindset, while fewer than half of the students in Mexico, Poland, and Hong Kong did.

Here's an important piece of the puzzle, though: having a growth mindset isn't just about believing you can improve. It's also about having a supportive environment that fuels that belief. This is where your teachers or mentors come in. Studies show that having supportive teachers— the kind who care about every student's learning and offer extra help—makes you more likely to develop a growth mindset. And in the U.S., students with this mindset and supportive teachers did exceptionally well in reading—outshining those with a fixed mindset by a whopping 72 points.

So, what's the big idea behind all this, and why should you care about this book? Here's the thing: we're living in a world where school stress, social media comparisons, and even global situations like the pandemic are constant challenges. And handling these challenges has a lot to do with the type of mindset we have. A growth mindset can help us tackle these tests of resilience, learn from our mistakes, and lead more fulfilled lives. This book is here to help you cultivate that mindset and to guide you in creating an environment that nurtures it. Ready to discover the power of a growth mindset?

Why this book and not other growth mindset books?

You might be thinking, "why this book? Aren't there already a bunch of books on growth mindset out there?" You're right! There are indeed tons of books on this topic. And believe me, I've dived into a fair share of them. Here's what I found:

1. Many of these books are filled with a lot of theoretical stuff and jargon, but don't offer a lot of practical, in-the-moment techniques you can use.

2. Some books present complicated strategies that either feel too over-whelming for a teen or seem to require a psychologist to decipher. It's like trying to build a spaceship without an instruction manual.

3. Other books have some genuinely good advice, but the info doesn't stick. You read it, feel inspired, and then... poof! A week later, you can't remember what you read, and you haven't really changed anything in your day-to-day life.

Don't get me wrong, there are some fantastic resources out there. But when I decided to share what i'd learned about nurturing a growth mindset, I wanted to provide you with a **game-changing, habit-forming resource.** I wanted to create something that would resonate with you and offer tangible strategies that I found truly effective.

What sets this book apart is our unique 50-Day Program designed to make

the growth mindset a way of life. Not only will we be exploring the concept and benefits of a growth mindset, but we'll also guide you in making it a habit and offer tools and resources to help you maintain and improve your mindset.

In essence, this book is a real-deal resource, written by someone who's been in your shoes, made the journey, and is now committed to helping you make the most of your own journey.

How to use this book?

Welcome to your epic adventure—*The Essential Growth Mindset Handbook for Teens*. This is your go-to guide, filled to the brim with eleven awesome chapters, each packed with juicy info, practical stuff to do, and real-life experiences that make the whole growth mindset thing super interesting.

Chapter 1 is your VIP pass into the cool world of mindsets. We're going to tackle the differences between a fixed and a growth mindset. Plus, there's a bit where you can find out more about your own mindset—pretty neat, right?

Chapter 2 is all about the crazy-awesome teen brain. Get ready to dip your toes into the sea of neuroscience and learn how it links up with your mindset.

In Chapter 3, we're gonna chat about the real power of belief. You'll see how switching up your beliefs can totally change your life. We'll take a look at some superstars who made big changes using the power of a growth mindset.

Next up, Chapter 4 is all about changing the way you think about failure. With some super cool exercises, this chapter will help you see failure as a stepping stone, not a dead end.

Chapters 5, 6, and 7 are your guide to using a growth mindset in all parts of your life. Whether it's school, friendships, or sports, we've got tons of advice, stories, and tools to keep you pumped and focused.

Chapter 8 is all about setting goals. Here, you'll get your hands on some killer strategies, fun templates, and a toolkit to make sure your goals line up with the growth mindset way of thinking.

In Chapter 9, we're gonna talk about the connection between a growth mindset, mental health, and how you feel overall. Look forward to expert advice, mindfulness exercises that you'll actually want to try, and lots of resources to help you along your mental health journey.

Chapter 10 is super exciting. This is the start of your 50-day growth mindset revolution! This day-by-day plan will really help you nail down the principles of the growth mindset.

Then we have **Chapter 11,** which keeps the growth energy flowing with tips on visualization, journaling, affirmations, and more.

And for your parents, we've got a chapter so they can get in on the action and support your growth mindset journey. They'll find conversation starters, ways to handle challenges, and a toolkit of their own.

And it doesn't stop at the chapters! At the end of the book, we've put together some really useful resources—Ted Talks, videos, books, movies, documentaries, websites, and tools. These are going to be super helpful to supplement what you learn from the book. We've given you a summary on each one, so you can pick and choose what you think will help you the most.

Feel free to jump around the chapters, pick what catches your eye first, but make sure you really get into it—that's how you'll get the most out of this book. Share this journey with a friend, a mentor, or a counselor, but remember it's your journey. Keep it flexible and take it one step at a time.

Ready to kick-start your growth mindset journey? Let's get moving!

IT'S A JOURNEY

CHAPTER 1

Understanding the Growth Mindset

Mindset. You've probably heard that word tossed around a ton like it's the secret key to unlocking some mystical treasure. Well, let's get real about it. Imagine, you're wrestling with this gnarly math problem, it's giving you the stink eye and you're seriously considering setting your textbook on fire. That feeling? That's your mindset peeking through.

STINK EYE

What's a mindset, you ask? Picture your mindset as this massive collage of your thoughts and beliefs about stuff—how you see the world and interpret all the wild, whacky, and wonderful things that happen to you. It's like your life-filter, adding its own unique shade to every experience you have—good, bad, and everything in between.

But here's the thing, your mindset isn't just lounging in your brain. Nope, it's busy at work, shaping your life. It's like the secret boss of your life's video game, calling the shots and deciding which level you're gonna face next.

Say you're gunning for student council president. If you're convinced you're gonna lose (ahem, that's a fixed mindset), you might not go all-in on your campaign, you could lose hope quickly, and in the end, miss out on the crown.

But if you believe that you can amp up your game with a little elbow grease and take criticism on the chin (hey there, growth mindset!), You're more likely to throw yourself into the campaign, learn from the feedback, and level up. Winning might not be a cakewalk, but you've got a good shot.

SUCCESS!

PERSISTENCE

LEARNING
FROM
FEEDBACK

PERSISTENCE

PRACTICE

EFFORT

CHALLENGE

That's the magic of mindset. It molds your actions, shapes your experiences, and ultimately, writes your life story. Awesome, right?

So, your mindset? It can guide you toward growth, discovery, and learning, or it can have you driving in circles, feeling stuck. The best part? You're in the driver's seat. You get to pick the route.

Imagine being able to tap into this superpower to make your teenage years even more epic. Well, that's precisely what this book is all about. You're about to learn how to harness the power of your mindset and steer your life in the direction of your dreams.

Growth mindset vs. fixed mindset

Alright, now that we've broken down what a 'mindset' is, let's unpack two big players in this field: the growth mindset and the fixed mindset. Think of these two as the ultimate rivals in how you view yourself and the world. Understanding them is kind of a big deal for navigating your teen years and beyond.

What does a growth mindset look like?

Imagine you're trying to learn skateboarding. If you're team growth mindset, you believe that with patience, practice, and persistence, you'll be pulling off ollies and kickflips in no time. You're down to work hard, tackle those hard tricks, and learn from each time you stumble or fall. Stumbles aren't your enemy; they're your teachers, guiding your path to shredding it at the skatepark.

 In a nutshell, if you have a growth mindset, you view abilities as things that can be developed, like muscles at a gym. You believe in the power of the word 'yet.' Maybe you can't land a kickflip YET, but you know you'll get there with time and practice.

And a fixed mindset?

Switching gears, if you're hanging out with the fixed mindset crew, you think your abilities are set in stone, like a mountain that can't be moved. Going back to the skateboard scenario: if you're in the fixed mindset zone, you might say, "I'm just not cut out for skateboarding. I'll never get the hang of this," almost immediately.

In the fixed mindset realm, it's all about absolutes: you're either a natural at something or you're not. And if you're not? Well, a fixed mindset whispers that there's no point in trying because no amount of practice will make a difference.

With a growth mindset, you're ready to face challenges head-on, stick it out when things get tough, and understand that putting in the effort is part of the journey to mastery. This mindset is your passport, leading you toward new experiences and achievements.

On the other hand, a fixed mindset might make you dodge challenges, tap out when things get difficult, and see effort as a waste of time. This mindset can act like an anchor, holding you back from sailing toward your potential and tasting the richness life has to offer.

Keep in mind, you're in control here. You hold the power to shape your mindset, and in doing so, craft your life's adventure. This book is your guide to fostering a growth mindset, opening up a universe of possibilities.

Importance of developing a growth mindset

Here's the million-dollar question: why should you care about this growth mindset? Well, having a growth mindset is like finding a secret portal in a video game. It doesn't guarantee an easy ride, but it sure helps you handle the game's challenges with style. Let's unpack this a bit.

Learning & problem-solving skills: From meh to yeah!

A growth mindset can take your learning and problem-solving abilities to a whole new level. Here's the thing, with a growth mindset, you're not terrified of messing up or diving into uncharted waters. Why? Because that's where the real learning goes down. This attitude can morph you into a problem-solving whiz. Math problem acting all high and mighty? Bring it on! With a growth mindset, you'll treat it as an opportunity, not a roadblock.

Rise and shine after a tumble

Next up is resilience—that nifty skill of springing back when life knocks you down. Having a growth mindset is like having a resilience guru in your corner. It's not about living a fail-proof life (spoiler: everyone trips up), but about knowing how to pick yourself up, learn from the experience, and keep marching forward. In the world of growth mindset, failure isn't an end but a pit stop on your highway to success.

Emotional and mental health: Got that covered!

And here's a big one. A growth mindset is like a secret weapon for your emotional and mental well-being. It nudges you towards self-compassion, patience, and a glass-half-full approach, which can help keep stress and anxiety at bay. And, since a growth mindset treats obstacles as launchpads, it can also ramp up your confidence and happiness levels. It's like your very own mood enhancer!

The proof's in the pudding

Now you might be thinking, "sounds nice, but is it legit?" Oh, you bet! This isn't some pep rally talk, it's backed by tons of research. Studies show that folks with a growth mindset are more likely to reach their goals, cope better with stress, and even maintain healthier relationships.

The brains behind this concept, Dr. Carol Dweck, found that students who embraced a growth mindset saw their abilities as something they could expand with a bit of elbow grease. They welcomed challenges, learned from criticism, and were inspired by others' wins. As for students with a fixed mindset? Not quite the same story. So, all this growth mindset buzz? It's not hot air. It's science-backed.

To sum up, embracing a growth mindset can be like flipping on your life's "epic mode" switch. It's not just about doing better—it's about living better.

Growth mindset and the teenage years

Hey, let's face it. The teen years can be a wild roller coaster. It's like you're in a constant state of motion (and sometimes even chaos!)—Navigating school stuff, friendships, self-discovery, and future plans. It's kinda thrilling, but also a bit daunting, right? But, listen up! Your teen years are an amazing time to start harnessing the power of a growth mindset. You see, your brain during these years is pretty much like an eager student, ready to learn and adapt.

By embracing a growth mindset now, you're giving yourself an epic toolkit for all the stuff that comes next—college, work, and adulting in general. Think of it as investing in a superpower early on so you're ready to conquer whatever comes your way.

 Your teen years are all about discovering who you are. You might be wondering, "what am I passionate about? Where do my strengths lie? What kind of person am I becoming?" It's like you're painting a self-portrait, and each experience adds a new color. With a growth mindset, you're able to see yourself as a masterpiece in progress. You'll learn to view your strengths and weaknesses not as permanent traits, but areas that can bloom with effort and patience. It's like granting yourself the freedom to grow and change.

Now, let's talk school. Exams, grades, projects, maybe even prepping for college. It's like a high-stakes juggling act. But here's the good news: a growth mindset can help you ace this performance. It helps you view challenges as opportunities to learn and grow, not as terrifying monsters. It teaches you to stay curious, keep pushing, and know that a single test or grade doesn't define your worth. So, academic pressure? With a growth mindset, you're all, "challenge accepted."

And then there's the social stuff. Friends, cliques, navigating social media—it feels like a crazy labyrinth sometimes. But a growth mindset can light the way. It promotes empathy, understanding, and resilience, helping you build stronger, healthier relationships. Plus, it reminds you that everyone's journey is unique, and it's totally okay to follow your own path. So, even when social situations seem like a maze, a growth mindset can be your trusty map.

In essence, adopting a growth mindset can be an absolute game-changer during your teenage years. It's not just a new way of thinking—it's a toolkit, a guide, and a trustworthy companion. And the best part? It's all within your reach.

Transitioning from a fixed mindset to a growth mindset

So, you're thinking: "this growth mindset stuff sounds great, but how do I actually change the way I think?" It's a legit question. Switching up your mindset is a bit like learning a new language or mastering a cool skateboard trick. It takes practice, patience, and a willingness to mess up and dust yourself off when things don't go quite as planned.

Your mindset is like your world filter. With a fixed mindset, you might see the world in a "what you see is what you get" kind of way. As if your skills and abilities are set in stone, and you just have to roll with what you've got.

But slide on a growth mindset, and suddenly, things start to look different. You begin to see that with some hard work and determination, you can actually stretch and grow your abilities. You're not stuck where you are—you can level up.

And here's the really cool part: this isn't just some kind of magical thinking. People actually do this! **It's not like you'll never face struggles again. But when you do, you'll be way more equipped to take them on, learn from them, and come out the other side stronger.**

Real talk: stories of mindset switch-ups

Okay, enough theory. Let's get down to the real world. There are plenty of folks out there who've done the whole fixed-to-growth mindset switcheroo. Want some inspiration? Here it is:

Remember Michael Jordan? You know, the all-star basketball player? His road to fame wasn't a piece of cake. Dude got dropped from his high school basketball team because he was 'too short'! But did he throw in the towel? Nope. He worked harder, practiced more, and proved them wrong. As he once said, **"I've missed more than 9,000 shots in my career... I've failed over and over and over again in my life. And that is why I succeed."** That, my friends, is a growth mindset in action.

And what about J.K. Rowling? Ever heard of her? She wrote a little series called Harry Potter. But before her magical world took off, Rowling got the big old 'no' from multiple publishers. Some folks might've taken that as a sign they weren't cut out for the job. But not J.K. She kept on writing, didn't give up, and... well, you know the rest.

The moral of these stories? They're not about folks who had an easy ride to the top. They're about people who hit bumps in the road, maybe even fell flat on their faces, but didn't let that stop them. They saw failures not as full stops, but as stepping stones to success. It's real-life proof that switching from a fixed mindset to a growth mindset isn't just doable—it's downright transformative.

Mindset self-assessment

Alright, let's do a bit of exploring, shall we? Picture this quiz as your flashlight, helping you discover what's currently chilling in the corners of your mind. Read each question, and pick the option that you relate to the most. There are no wrong answers here, promise.

1. **When you're confronted with a mega-difficult problem, what's your move?**

A. Throw in the towel. If it's not clicking now, it's probably a lost cause.

B. Buckle down. Each problem is like a Rubik's Cube just waiting to be solved.

2. **Say someone hands you a hefty slice of criticism pie. How does that make you feel?**

A. Honestly, kind of attacked. It feels like they're telling me I'm not up to snuff.

B. Curious. I ponder their words and consider how I can level up from them.

3. **When you flop at something...**

A. It's clear to me that I'm simply not built for it.

B. I see it as a lesson in disguise. What can I do differently next time?

4. **If you're not instantly nailing it...**

A. I'd prefer to steer clear.

B. Bring it on. I'm psyched to learn, even if I fail a few times along the way.

5. **When you spot someone who's aceing something you're struggling with...**

A. I get a little green with envy. It's a harsh reminder of my limitations.

B. It gets my gears going. They're living proof of what's achievable with a little grit.

6. How do you feel about stepping out of your comfort zone?

A. I'd rather not, thanks. It's called a comfort zone for a reason.

B. I see it as an adventure. It's an opportunity to grow and discover new things.

7. When it comes to intelligence, do you think...

A. You're born with a certain amount, and that's it.

B. It's like a muscle—the more you exercise it, the stronger it gets.

8. What's your view on effort?

A. It's pointless if you're not naturally good at something.

B. It's key to mastering any skill or challenge.

9. How do you react when you see a peer doing better than you?

A. It feels like a slap in the face. I should be at their level.

B. It's motivating! If they can do it, so can I.

10. What's your stance on failure?

A. It's the universe's way of saying I shouldn't bother.

B. It's not the end of the world—it's a stepping stone towards success.

Answer key

Mostly As: your responses suggest you might be hanging out in fixed mindset territory right now. You seem to see abilities as static and setbacks might feel like giant walls.

Mostly Bs: your responses suggest you're more in the growth mindset camp. You seem to see obstacles as opportunities and believe that, with some sweat and elbow grease, you can always improve.

Remember, this isn't about "passing" or "failing"—it's about getting to know your mindset better. **If you're rocking a fixed mindset vibe, don't freak out.** The thing about mindsets is they're not like a tattoo—they're more like a pencil sketch. And with some effort, you can definitely do some editing.

For those sporting a fixed mindset: change is coming

Just in case you're sitting there thinking "oh man, I'm all fixed mindset, what do I do now?"—Don't sweat it. The very fact that you're here, taking this quiz, and reading this book means you're open to change. And guess what? That's a growth mindset in action right there.

See, the awesome thing about mindsets is that they're not set in stone. They're more like Play-Doh. With a little work, you can mold and shape them into something new. Yes, even you fixed-mindset folks out there. Especially you, in fact.

Remember, this isn't about becoming someone else. It's about becoming the best version of yourself. So, buckle up, because we're about to dive into how you can nurture your growth mindset and transform the way you approach challenges, failures, and successes.

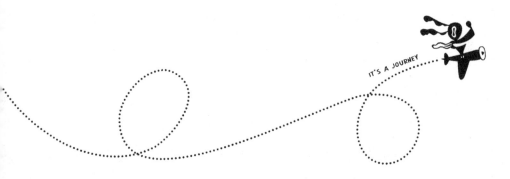

IT'S A JOURNEY

CHAPTER 2

Understanding the Teenage Brain

Alright, so why are we starting our deep dive into the growth mindset with a tour of the teenage brain? Well, it's kinda like trying to be a whiz at using a super high-tech gadget without understanding how it works—not exactly a recipe for success, right?

The same goes for your brain. If you want to unlock its full potential and cultivate a growth mindset, you gotta get the basics of what's happening up there. Not to freak you out or anything, but your brain is actually going through some pretty wild changes during your teenage years. It's reshaping, rewiring, and getting ready to power you through some of the most exciting times of your life.

The good news? Understanding these changes and how they impact your thoughts and behaviors is like scoring a cheat sheet to ace the game. It's gonna give you that extra edge to nurture your growth mindset and, not to overhype it or anything, but kinda shape your own destiny.

So, buckle up, brainiacs! It's time to take a thrilling trip into the remarkable world of the teenage brain. No jargon, no snooze-fests, just the need-to-knows delivered straight up.

The marvel of the brain

The brain. That three-pound marvel that's basically the boss of your body. It's the ultimate control room, handling everything from your deepest thoughts to your wildest emotions, even that tickle in your toe. It's always buzzing, always working, making you, well, you. All your dreams, all your hopes, even that song stuck in your head, it's all thanks to your brain.

Simplified explanation of the brain's structure: the key parts and their roles

Let's zoom in for a closer look. Your brain isn't just one big lump of grey stuff; it's got different parts, each with its own special job.

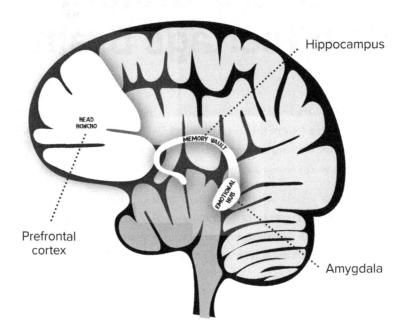

The **prefrontal cortex,** for instance, it's like the brain's head honcho. It helps you plan, make decisions, and understand others' feelings. That thing you did the other day, thinking twice before eating the last slice of pizza because you knew your sister would be upset? Yup, that was your prefrontal cortex doing its thing.

Then there's the **amygdala,** the emotional hub of your brain. Feel like crying at that movie or laughing at that meme? Your amygdala's got your back.

And let's not forget the **hippocampus,** your personal memory vault. It helps you store and retrieve memories, like that secret handshake you have with your bestie.

Intriguing facts about the teenage brain

Okay, time for some brainy trivia! Did you know that your brain makes up only about 2% of your body's weight, but uses up about 20% of its energy? Talk about high maintenance!

Or how about this? As a teenager, your brain is undergoing a huge renovation. It's reorganizing, optimizing, and becoming more efficient. It's like your brain is upgrading from a regular phone to a smartphone, getting ready to perform even better. So, all that drama and emotion you sometimes feel? It's part of your brain's growth spurt. Don't worry, it's all part of the plan.

Basic neuroscience for teens

Let's crack open the hood and check out the mechanics of the brain. Don't worry, it won't be like that dull biology class you almost snoozed in. This is all about you and what's happening in your brain right now.

What happens to the brain during adolescence: the science behind the growth and changes

So, being a teenager means being right in the middle of a mind-blowing transformation. Your brain is basically under construction. Picture this, all the circuits in your brain are being fine-tuned, pruned, and re-wired to make it faster, sharper, and much more efficient. This process starts at the back of your brain and slowly works its way to the front.

You know that prefrontal cortex we mentioned? Well, it's the last part to get the upgrade. That's why, sometimes, making decisions or thinking things through might feel a bit like trying to solve a Rubik's Cube blindfolded. But don't worry, it's all part of the grand plan, and it does get easier. Promise!

Hormonal changes and their effects on the brain and behavior

Now, onto the hormones. As a teen, you're riding a hormonal roller coaster. These hormones don't just cause the occasional zit or voice crack, they also play a huge part in how your brain develops.

Hormones like testosterone and estrogen kick-start the growth of your brain during puberty. They help forge new connections between brain cells and rein-force existing ones. These changes can affect how you think, learn, and even how you interact with others. So, if you're feeling all over the place sometimes, know that it's normal and part of this epic journey you're on.

The role of sleep in brain development and the effects of sleep deprivation

Lastly, let's talk about something we all love: sleep. It's not just a great excuse to cozy up in your blankets, it also plays a crucial role in your brain's development.

While you're lost in dreamland, your brain is surprisingly active. It's using this downtime to strengthen new connections and get rid of the ones you no longer need. It's like your brain's version of taking out the trash and organizing your room.

 But what if you're missing out on some z's? Well, sleep deprivation can make it harder to focus, learn new stuff, or even manage your mood. So, think twice before pulling that all-nighter to binge-watch your favorite show. Your brain needs its beauty sleep, too!

Neuroplasticity: the brain's superpower

Ready for another round of mind-blowing science? Today's menu features a special dish called 'neuroplasticity.' I know it sounds like it's straight out of a sci-fi movie, right? Let's unpack this brainy superpower.

Neuroplasticity might sound like some alien technology, but it's actually a pretty cool feature of your own brain. Think of your brain as a megacity with roads and pathways connecting different parts. Now, imagine if that city could create new roads, change existing ones, or even upgrade highways as needed. That's neuroplasticity! Your brain reshapes its 'roads' to help you learn and adapt.

Neuroplasticity in action: it's everywhere!

Alright, so where can you spot neuroplasticity doing its thing? Just about everywhere! Picked up a few Spanish phrases for your trip to Mexico? That's neuroplasticity. Mastered that tricky guitar solo? Neuroplasticity again! Moved to a new town and learned to navigate the local transit system? Yep, you guessed it, more neuroplasticity!

Even when things don't go as planned, like tripping and spraining your ankle, neuroplasticity jumps into action. It helps your brain work around the problem until you're back on your feet (literally).

Boosting your brain's superpower

Okay, so now you know that your brain has this awesome power. How do you make it even more powerful? Just like superheroes need training to hone their powers, your brain needs some workout too.

First off, learning is your brain's favorite exercise. It doesn't have to be all big and serious like cracking calculus problems. Even fun stuff like learning a new dance routine or mastering a new video game can help.

Next, keep moving. Yup, good old physical exercise does wonders for your brain too. It helps your brain stay fit and sharp.

Lastly, don't forget to rest. Just like your body, your brain needs downtime to recharge. So, get enough sleep, try some relaxing mindfulness practices, or simply enjoy some quiet moments to yourself.

Just remember, your brain is ever-changing, ever-adapting, just like you. And that's truly something to marvel at.

Mindset and the brain: an intriguing connection

Your brain is a pretty complex piece of machinery, but here's an interesting twist: your mindset can play a big role in how it works. Picture your brain like a top-tier athlete. It's trained, it's fit, it's ready to roll. But, what happens if that athlete starts doubting their abilities? Their performance dips, right? Even if their physical fitness hasn't changed a bit.

Your mindset works in a similar way to your brain. The things you believe about yourself can shape how your brain performs its tasks, how it learns, and how it reacts to challenges.

Science says: mindset matters

Now, we're not just saying this for fun. There's actual science backing it up. Let's talk about an exciting area of research, called cognitive neuroscience. Big name, I know, but it's all about studying how our thoughts and attitudes can change our brains.

IT'S SCIENCE

Experiments have shown that people with a growth mindset—that's those who believe they can improve and learn—actually react differently to challenges. Their brains stay engaged, lighting up with activity, even when things get tough. But those who think they can't improve? Their brains tend to check out as soon as things get difficult. So, what you think about your abilities can literally change how your brain works.

It's not just a one-way street though. Your brain also plays a big part in shaping your mindset. Think about it. Your brain is like the command center, right? It's receiving and sending out signals all the time. Those signals form your beliefs, your thoughts, and yes, your mindset.

That's where neuroplasticity comes back into play. Remember our brain's superpower? Yep, it means your mindset can change. Your brain can adapt, and so can your beliefs about yourself. The brain's flexibility gives us a chance to shift our mindset, learn, and grow.

Your thoughts and beliefs have power—the power to shape your brain and the power to change your life. So, keep that in mind as you journey through this growth mindset adventure!

Fun brain teasers: your turn to shine

Now, let's put all that knowledge to use with some interactive puzzles and brain teasers. No pressure, they're just for fun. But hey, they might give your neuro-plasticity a little boost. You'll find the answer key in the resources chapter right at the end of the book.

1. The brainy word unscramble
Time to test those language skills and fast-thinking neurons. Try to unscramble these brain-related words. Remember, no internet help, we're testing your brain, not your search engine skills!

NARIB (hint: it's where it all happens)

AAMIGYDL (hint: it's all about your emotions)

TYPINICASRLEUO (hint: your brain's awesome superpower!)

2. The memory maze

This one's a quick memory test. We're going to list a few items. Read through them 5 times, then close your eyes and see how many you can remember. No peeking!

Elephant   Skateboard   Banana   Telescope   Toothbrush   Watermelon

3. Think quick!

Test your response time and creativity with this one. I'll start a sentence, and you've gotta end it with the first thing that comes to your mind. Remember, it's about being quick, not perfect!

- If I could talk to my brain, I would say...
- The coolest thing about my brain is...
- If I could give my brain a superpower, it would be...

4. The brainy crossword

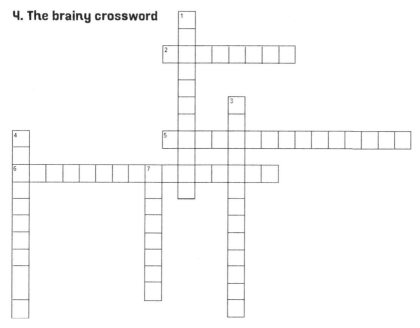

ACROSS

2. This is the 'feel good' neurotransmitter.
5. The term for the brain's ability to change and adapt.
6. This part of the brain helps you with decision making and controling impulses.

DOWN

1. This period of life is when the brain undergoes significant changes.
3. This term describes your belief in your ability to grow and improve.
4. This part of your brain helps with memory and learning.
7. This almond-shaped part of your brain helps process your emotions.

5. Visual puzzle

This one's for all the visual thinkers out there. Below is an image with several objects and people and animals hidden in it. How many can you find?

Source: https://www.Behance.Net/gallery/81562393/hidden-objects-illustrations

6. The 'what comes next' challenge

Can you figure out the pattern and tell what comes next?

Pattern 1: 3, 6, 12, 21, __?__

Pattern 2: 4, 8, 16, 28, __?__

Pattern 3: 5, 10, 20, 35, __?__

Now let's up the difficulty level!

Pattern 4: 2, 4, 12, 48, __?__

Pattern 5: 3, 9, 81, 2187, __?__

Pattern 6: 5, 25, 625, 9765625, __?__

7. Brainy riddles

Check out these brainy riddles. Can you solve them?

Riddle 1: I speak without a mouth and hear without ears. I have no body, but I come alive with the wind. What am I?

Riddle 2: You see me once in June, twice in February, and none in May. What am I?

Riddle 3: I have cities, but no houses. I have mountains, but no trees. I have water, but no fish. What am I?

Riddle 4: The more you take, the more you leave behind. What am I?

Riddle 5: I am taken from a mine and shut up in a wooden case, from which I am never released, and yet I am used by almost every person. What am I?

Riddle 6: I fly without wings, I cry without eyes. Wherever I go, darkness follows me. What am I?

Riddle 7: What can be broken, but is never held?

Riddle 8: I'm light as a feather, yet the strongest person can't hold me for five minutes. What am I?

Riddle 9: I am full of keys, but I can't open any door. What am I?

Riddle 10: I'm not alive, but I can grow; I don't have lungs, but I need air; I don't have a mouth, but water kills me. What am I?

Keep going, brainiac!

We're all on this journey together. So, remember, keep being curious, keep exploring. Our brains are like uncharted galaxies, with a ton of new things to discover. And everything you've learned about the growth mindset? Start using it. You'll be amazed at what you and your brain can do together.

CHAPTER 3

The Power of Belief

L et's get this straight: your beliefs about yourself have some serious clout. It's not just about deciding whether you'll crush it in Fortnite or have a killer day. The stakes are higher. Your beliefs are like the rudder to your life's ship, guiding your actions and choices. Your beliefs can either be your personal cheer squad, nudging you towards fresh experiences, or they can be the wet blankets, holding you back from opportunities.

Picture this: you've decided that math is as friendly as a porcupine. There's a good chance you'll give that electrifying advanced math class a miss or pass up a fantastic job prospect because it involves a bit of math wizardry. Your beliefs can either unlock doors or bolt them shut in your life. That's why it's mega-important to stay alert to the narratives you create about yourself.

Beliefs, risks, and opportunities

To add more layers to this, your beliefs also play a significant role in how much risk you're willing to take. You know, those exhilarating leaps of faith into the unknown. If you're buzzing with self-belief, you're more likely to take on the unexpected, like trying out for the school play or starting a youtube channel on that topic you're crazy about.

On the other hand, if you're bogged down by self-doubt, you might find yourself playing it safe, sticking to what you know, and sidestepping chances to explore something new. Now, playing it safe isn't always a bad thing, but when it stops you from stretching your limits and growing, it can be a bit of a downer.

Changing the story, changing the path

But here's the part that should get you pumped: you have the power to change this story. That's right. You get to decide what you believe about yourself. So, if you've been telling yourself that you're not cut out for math, art, or sports, or anything else, you have the chance right now to flip that script. The new narrative could be: "I'm not where I want to be yet in math (or art or sports), but I can get better with effort and practice." You see the difference? It's not about denying where you are but about recognizing where you could be.

Ready to reshape your beliefs and unlock new adventures? Let's dive deeper and discover how to harness the power of self-belief to boost your growth mindset.

The belief-health connection

Here's a twist you might not have seen coming: your beliefs about yourself aren't just influencing your opportunities and the decisions you make. They're also having a major effect on your health, both mental and physical. Sound a bit out there? Maybe, but once you chew on it a bit, it starts to make sense.

So, imagine you see yourself as someone who can tackle any challenge head-on. Even when you stumble or hit a speed bump, you're not likely to find yourself face-planting into despair. That means less stress and less stress means

 a happier you, both mentally and physically. Because, remember, your mind and your body? They're not just acquaintances; they're a power-packed team, always in each other's corners.

The stress-health equation: breaking it down

Let's break it down a bit more. We all know that stress is a bit of a buzzkill, right? It can lead to all sorts of nasty stuff, from sleepless nights to mood swings to a weaker immune system. Not fun. Now, imagine you're constantly telling yourself that you can't do things or that you're bound to fail. That's going to pile on the stress like nobody's business.

On the flip side, if you have a can-do attitude, if you believe in your ability to grow and improve, you're likely to handle stress better. You'll see setbacks not as catastrophes but as opportunities to learn and bounce back. It's like having your very own stress-busting superpower.

Emotional health and self-belief: the BFFs

Your beliefs also play a major role in your emotional health. Imagine believing that you're a lost cause every time you make a mistake. That would make you feel pretty crummy, right? But if you view mistakes as part of the learning process, you're more likely to maintain a positive outlook, even in the face of failure.

But don't just take our word for it. This isn't just pep talk or wishful thinking. Loads of scientific research backs this up. Studies have found that having a positive self-belief system can reduce the risk of depression, increase life satisfaction, and even enhance physical health. So, the belief-health connection isn't just about feeling good—it's about living better.

Let's jump into the nitty-gritty and learn how to tweak those beliefs for a supercharged growth mindset!

The super team: your brain and your beliefs

Pop quiz, hotshot: what's the most powerful tool you've got to navigate this wild ride we call life? If you said 'your brain', you're half right. But the full answer? It's your brain teamed up with your beliefs. Yeah, you heard right. Your beliefs—those core truths you hold about yourself and the world around you—are the sidekick to your brain's superhero, and together, they're a force to be reckoned with.

Remember when we talked about neuroplasticity? That's your brain's secret weapon, its uncanny ability to reshape and adapt itself based on what you're learning and experiencing. It's like your brain's a master builder, constantly revising its architectural plans to build a better, stronger, and more efficient version of you.

Now, imagine you're armed with a rock-solid belief that you're going to ace your next math exam or nail that tricky guitar solo you've been practicing. When you hold such powerful faith in your abilities and challenge yourself to go beyond your limits, your brain gets the memo. It's like you're whispering in your brain's ear, "hey, we've got this. Let's make it happen!" And your brain, being the loyal sidekick, gets to work.

But here's the real game-changer: your self-belief isn't just floating around in your head like a thought bubble in a comic. Nope, it's way more involved than that. It's like the co-pilot in your brain's cockpit, working hand in hand with your brain to drive your life toward your goals. It's like your

SELF BELIEF   **STRESS**

HOW SELF-BELIEF FIGHTS STRESS

beliefs and your brain are the dynamic duo of your life's adventure, charting the course that gets you where you want to go. Now, if that doesn't sound like an epic superhero team, I don't know what does.

Now, let's talk about two real-life superstars who embody the spirit of a growth mindset like nobody else. Notice how their beliefs about their abilities have shaped their hard-as-steel mindset.

Successful individuals and the growth mindset

The Madonna saga: turning "no" into "now"

We're talking about none other than the pop queen herself, Madonna. But don't think she was born with a silver spoon or a royal scepter in her hand. No way! Her journey to stardom was more rock-filled road than a red carpet.

Imagine being a young girl from Michigan, moving to the concrete jungle that is New York City, with only a handful of dollars and a big dream. Sounds exciting, sure, but it was also super tough. Madonna was hit with more rejection than a pimply nerd at a prom dance. People said she was too provocative, too different, too...well, Madonna.

The queen in making: facing rejections

But guess what? She didn't let any of that pull her down. Nope, instead, she strapped on her growth mindset like a pair of knee-high boots and strutted her way through every challenge. Every "no" was just a "not now," every rejection a call to work harder, every door slammed in her face an opportunity to find another way in.

A visionary: Madonna's success recipe

She believed in herself, her unique style, her outrageous creativity, and her untamed talent. She kept pushing, turning every stone, seeking every opportunity to hone her craft, experimenting with her music, and daring to be different. She danced in clubs, sang back-up, acted—anything and everything that got her closer to her dream.

And then, she was a Queen!

And look where that grit and tenacity got her! Today, she stands tall as a global icon, a multi-millionaire, and the undisputed Queen of Pop. Her music has evolved over the decades, continuously resonating with different generations. She's been a trailblazer, a rule-breaker, and above all, a relentless learner.

So, Madonna's story is proof that a growth mindset isn't just some theory. It's a real-life superpower that can take you from zero to hero. Remember, every rejection is an invitation to rise higher, and every setback is just a setup for a grand comeback!

Thomas Edison: the wizard of "not yet"

When we think of a growth mindset, it's not just limited to scoring goals on the football field or belting out chart-topping hits. In fact, it can shine even brighter in the realm of invention and innovation. Need an example? Well, let's beam some light on Thomas Edison—the genius inventor who revolutionized the world with his creation: the electric light bulb.

The rocky start

Edison's journey to light up the world wasn't as bright and shiny as you might think. Nope, it was a winding path with heaps of obstacles. If you're picturing a genius inventor coming up with a brilliant idea in a light bulb moment—pun totally intended—then you might want to adjust your vision.

You see, Edison didn't invent the perfect light bulb on his first try or even his fiftieth. It was not a one-and-done situation. He made not one, not a hundred, but thousands of unsuccessful attempts before he finally got it right.

But here's where the magic of a growth mindset flickered in. To Edison, these weren't "failures." Instead, he saw each unsuccessful attempt as a valuable lesson, a stepping stone toward his goal. He once said, "I have not failed. I've just found 10,000 ways that won't work." That, my friends, is a growth mindset in action!

Every time a filament blew up or a design flopped, Edison didn't toss his hands up and say, "guess I'm just not cut out to be an inventor." Nope, he rolled up his sleeves and dove right back into the problem, fueled by the belief that he was getting closer to the solution.

And guess what? His belief, resilience, and relentless pursuit of growth paid off. He eventually figured it out, creating a practical, long-lasting electric light bulb that revolutionized the world. His invention lit up homes, streets, and cities, transforming the way we live our lives.

Your light bulb moment

So, you see, Edison's journey was about way more than just inventing a light bulb. It's a shining example of how a growth mindset can turn every failure into a step toward success. It's about seeing every setback as a setup for a breakthrough. So the next time you stumble, remember edison's story, and remind yourself that you're just one step closer to your light bulb moment!

Growth mindset: the secret sauce

So, what's the common thread in all these stories? Each of these individuals faced setbacks. They had their fair share of struggles. But they never stopped believing in themselves. They had a growth mindset—they believed they could improve, learn, and overcome challenges. And that belief fueled their journey to success.

The big take-home message? Believing in yourself isn't just about feeling good or being positive. It's science, my friend. The belief we have in ourselves directly influences our behaviors, our decisions, and how our futures unfold. Our brains, those command centers of ours, are intricately involved in this. They are our allies, ready to adapt and change as we do.

But now, it's your turn to grab the baton. The journey is in your hands now. Take everything you've learned from this chapter, and make it work for you. Try to shift your mindset when you're faced with a challenge. Understand that it's okay to fail, and it's fantastic to learn. Dare to dream big, work towards it, and see how your brain and your belief in yourself can make it happen.

CHAPTER 4

The Role of Failure in Growth

Right, so, we've all been there. That dreaded 'F' on a test paper. Losing in a match. The heart-sinking moment of "Oops, I messed up." You know, in our society, failing has a bad rap. People see it as something awful and terrifying. They dread it, avoid it, and often, it's considered a sign of weakness or incapability.

But what if we told you it's time to rethink all of that? Like, seriously rethink.

Here's a wild thought—imagine looking at failure as a golden ticket, a rare invite to learn and grow. Sounds crazy? Well, it might not be as wild as you think.

Failure, as hard as it can be to swallow, can also be an incredible chance to learn. When you miss the mark, you gain the chance to evaluate, reflect, and discover the areas where you can improve. Yep, that's right! **You're not defined by your failures. You're defined by how you *react* to them.**

Studies and findings showing the positive aspects of failure

A study from Stanford University found that students who understood and learned from their failures showed better performance than those who simply felt bad about it. They were less stressed, more open to challenges, and had a higher motivation to learn. How cool is that?

Other research shows that embracing failures can lead to resilience, adaptability, and a growth mindset. In other words, when you dust yourself off and hop back on the horse after a fall, you're building your mental muscle.

So, let's dive into this journey of reimagining failure, shall we? You might just find that this new perspective changes your life in ways you never thought possible.

Shifting perspective: failure as opportunity

So, you're wondering, "how do I turn this epic facepalm moment into an opportunity?" Good question! It all starts with a shift in perspective. It's about rewiring how you think about and respond to failure. You need to see failure as a lesson, not as a life sentence. It's like getting lost on a road trip. You didn't fail to reach your destination; you just found a way that didn't work. And now you're one step closer to finding the path that will!

So how do you start seeing failure in this cool, new light? Here are some strategies:

1. **Embrace it:** Start seeing failure as a natural part of learning and growth. Nobody's perfect, and everybody messes up sometimes. It's human!

2. **Analyze it:** When you fail, take a step back and analyze what happened. What went wrong? What could you do differently next time? Use your failure as a learning tool.

3. **Fail forward:** Adopt the mindset of failing forward. This means using each failure as a stepping stone to progress and move toward your goals.

4. **Speak kindly to yourself:** Treat yourself with kindness and compassion when you fail. Encourage yourself just as you would a friend.

Remember, flipping the script on failure isn't a one-and-done deal. It's a journey, a habit you cultivate over time. But trust us, it's a journey well worth the effort!

The resilience factor: learning from failure

Put simply, resilience it's basically your 'bounce-back' ability, your inner super-hero power that helps you deal with life's knockouts. It's all about picking yourself up, dusting off, and charging ahead, even when the going gets tough. Now let's see how failure is actually your secret weapon to level up this superpower.

Yeah, you read that right. Failure is your friend (kind of). Imagine you're playing a super tricky video game. You know the drill—you play, you lose, you play again, and you lose again. But each time, you're learning, adapting, and getting better, right? That's exactly how failure works. Each stumble, each facepalm moment makes you stronger, helps you adapt, and prepares you for life's curveballs. It's like your resilience gym, helping you build up those mental muscles!

Ever heard of Bethany Hamilton? Pro surfer, a total legend, and oh yeah, she also happens to surf with one arm. Why? Because she lost the other one in a shark attack. Yikes! But did she let that stop her? Nope. She hit the waves just a month later and continued to compete. Talk about resilience!

So, remember guys, failure isn't a big scary monster. It's just a stepping stone, helping you build resilience and come back stronger.

The reframe: practical exercises to embrace failure

Ok, time for some action! Let's work on flipping the script on failure. Here's a mini-project for you. Think about a time you messed up or didn't quite hit the mark, got it? Now, take a piece of paper and divide it into three columns.

In the first column, write down what happened—just the facts, no judgment. In the second, jot down how you felt about it—be honest, it's just you here. Now, here comes the magic. In the third column, list what you've learned from that experience, what it taught you, or how it helped you grow. Yep, that's right. We're literally turning failure into a teacher!

Here's an example:

The situation

Remember that math test you were really dreading? The one with all those perplexing algebraic expressions and equations? You studied hard for it, but when the results came back, it wasn't the score you were hoping for. You failed.

The facts, feelings, and the learning

Take a sheet of paper and divide it into three columns.

In the first column, jot down the facts. Here's an example:

- **Fact:** "I studied for two hours the night before the test, but I still failed."

In the second column, note down how you felt when you saw your score. Be as honest as you can, remember, this is just for you. Here's a possible entry:

- **Feeling:** "I felt disappointed and frustrated. I thought studying hard guaranteed a good grade, and I felt stupid when I failed."

Now for the third column, where the magic happens. We're going to transform this setback into a stepping stone. Think about what this experience taught you, how it helped you grow, or what it highlighted for you to work on. Here's a possible reflection:

- **Learning:** "I learned that cramming all my studying into one night may not be the most effective strategy for me. Next time, I'll try breaking up my study sessions over a few days. It also highlighted that I struggle with algebra, so I might seek some extra help to understand it better."

See what we did there? You took a failure and turned it into a lesson. This is the power of a growth mindset. It's not about never failing; it's about learning and growing from each experience. So, keep this reframing exercise in your toolkit, and remember, each stumble is just another step forward on your journey to becoming the best version of you. Now, that's some real superhero stuff right there!

LIKE A SUPERHERO

Turning setbacks into comebacks: the inspirational journey of Steve Jobs

Let's take a look at the epic tale of Steve Jobs, the dude behind Apple Inc. You know, the company that made that iPhone in your hand! His life's journey was a crazy roller-coaster ride that was anything but smooth.

At 30, Jobs faced a massive blow. He got kicked out of Apple, the company he'd built from scratch. Imagine that! It was as public as it was crushing, and to be honest, a lot of people thought that was the end of the road for him. Even Jobs himself felt pretty low and lost.

But did he let that define him? Heck no! Instead of throwing in the towel, Jobs chose to turn this massive failure into a stepping-stone for growth. He decided to, what we like to call, "fail forward."

The next five years saw him launching two new ventures: Next and Pixar. Next, a computer platform development outfit had a rocky start, and many thought it was the final nail in the coffin. But Jobs wasn't about to give up. He tweaked his products, learned from his mistakes, and kept moving. Pixar, on the other hand, went off like a rocket, creating "Toy Story," the first-ever entirely computer-animated film.

Here's where things take an unexpected twist. Apple buys Next, and Jobs comes back to his old stomping ground, this time armed with a boatload of experience from his time at Next and Pixar. This comeback was epic, and it led to Apple releasing some seriously cool stuff like the iPod, iPhone, and iPad.

In 2005, Jobs gave a killer speech to Stanford grads, where he looked back at his wild ride: "I didn't see it then, but it turned out that getting fired from Apple was the best thing that could have ever happened to me. The heaviness of being successful was replaced by the lightness of being a beginner again, less sure about everything. It freed me to enter one of the most creative periods of my life."

Jobs' story is the real-life version of "failing forward." That first bump in the road wasn't a stop sign—it was part of his journey to success. His experience taught him valuable lessons, made him stronger, and set him up to shake the tech industry. His story is a shoutout to all of us: embrace your failures, learn from them, and see them as steps to reach your goals.

Growth mindset in action

Inspired? We hope so! It's not about replicating someone else's journey. Your path is unique to you. Your failures, your lessons, and your growth—they're all yours. The key is to take the plunge, embrace failure, and see where it leads you. Just imagine the possibilities when you're not held back by the fear of failing. It's pretty awesome, isn't it?

Start by identifying a failure in your life. Big or small, it doesn't matter. Think about what you learned from it. How did it help you grow? How did it make you stronger or wiser? Then, practice this. With every failure you encounter, reframe it, learn from it, grow from it. Over time, you'll notice a change. You'll start to become more resilient, more open to new experiences, and more excited to learn.

Remember, it's not about being perfect; it's about becoming the best version of you. Embrace your unique journey, face your failures, and let's make magic happen!

IT'S A JOURNEY

CHAPTER 5

The Power of Growth mindset in Education and School

What if I told you that there's a secret ingredient to doing better in school? Would you believe me if I said it's all in your mind? Hold up, don't roll your eyes just yet. This isn't some magical Hogwarts stuff we're talking about, but the power of a growth mindset. And guess what? This magic lies within you.

Let's get this straight. A growth mindset is a belief that your abilities can develop with effort and practice. It's about understanding that smarts aren't

just something you're born with, but something you can build. Like working out to get those biceps popping, your brain can pump some iron too! In fact, treating your brain as a muscle is a pretty great way to look at it.

When we talk about 'learning as exercise', what we really mean is that every time you learn something new, your brain gets a little stronger. Each fact you memorize, every math problem you solve, every essay you write... they're all like a mini-workout session for your brain. And just like going to the gym, the more you work out (or in this case, learn), the stronger you get.

Sound interesting? Good, because understanding this is game-changing! Especially when it comes to your time in school. As it turns out, students who rock a growth mindset are more likely to crush their academic goals. And hey, who doesn't want that?

So buckle up, because we're about to learn how a growth mindset can significantly level up your academic game. We're talking about better grades, less stress, and an overall killer approach to your education.

Harnessing a growth mindset for academics

Alright, we've established that a growth mindset can seriously amp up your school game. But the burning question remains, how do we actually make it happen in real-life situations? How do we go from being a growth mindset believer to a growth mindset achiever?

Let's break it down. Say you're struggling with algebra, and you just can't seem to figure out those pesky equations. Now, if you were in a fixed mindset, you might think, "I'm just not good at math, I'll never get it." But hold up, remember that gym analogy we talked about earlier? Just like your muscles, your brain can grow, and you can get better at math.

Instead of letting your struggles pin you down, imagine saying to yourself, **"alright, algebra's tough for me right now, but that doesn't mean I'll never understand it. I just need to keep practicing."** And just like that, you've switched gears and you're in the growth mindset zone.

And hey, this isn't just about math. It applies to every subject you're studying, every project you're tackling, and even those monster-sized essays you have to write. Struggling with English literature? Can't get your head around those scientific concepts? No sweat, your brain's got this. Remember, it's not about not being able to do something; **it's about not being able to do it *yet*.**

Don't get me wrong, switching to a growth mindset isn't about ignoring the fact that things are hard. Nah, it's about acknowledging that yes, things can be challenging, but that doesn't define your abilities. Just think of each struggle as a brain workout, a chance for you to get a little stronger and a little better.

Using a growth mindset to reframe your academic struggles isn't about tricking yourself into thinking everything is rosy. **It's about seeing challenges for what they really are—opportunities to learn, to grow, and to get closer to being the best version of you.** Because every time you step out of your

RIGHT THIS WAY

comfort zone, even if it's hard, even if it doesn't go perfectly, you're still lapping everyone sitting on the couch! So flex that growth mindset and let's keep moving forward, one challenge at a time.

Strategies for conquering academic challenges

Now, let's dive into some hands-on strategies to give you the upper hand.

First off, we've got the "power of yet." Struggling with a complex math equation? You haven't solved it... *yet*. Can't quite nail down an essay topic? You haven't wrapped your head around it... *yet*. The trick here is to see your challenges as pesky speed bumps, not gigantic walls.

Meet Lucy. Chemistry was giving her a hard time. Her first thought was, "I'm totally lost. This stuff makes zero sense." But then she latched onto the "Power of Yet." She started telling herself, "Okay, this chemistry problem doesn't make sense *yet*, but if I keep at it, it will." And guess what? It did.

Next up, we've got the "learning from mistakes" strategy. Think of it as a secret weapon that lets you turn all your goof-ups into learning gold mines, rather than depressing measures of your smarts or skills. So, when you bomb a test, instead of beating yourself up, take a step back, analyze your errors, understand where you tripped up, and boom, you're armed to avoid the same mistakes in the future.

Take Alex, for example. He didn't do so well on a history test, and he was feeling pretty low. But instead of wallowing in self-pity, he turned it into a learning moment. He dissected each wrong answer, hunted down the right ones, and transformed that test into a killer study guide. The result? He totally crushed it next time around!

And last but definitely not least, we can "celebrate small wins." With all our focus zoomed in on the grand prize, we often forget the little wins that get us there. Each little progress you make, each tiny triumph, shows you're on the right track. So, take a moment to give yourself some credit. You deserve it!

Jenny was daunted by reading books and set a big goal to read 20 books in a year. It seemed like climbing Everest at first, but instead of getting freaked out, she celebrated each book she completed with her favorite self-care routine. Each book was a small victory, and by the end of the year, she had a collection of wins that added up to her smashing her goal!

Remember, having a growth mindset isn't about nailing everything perfectly; it's about striving for progress, not perfection. So, whether you're wrestling with a tricky subject, prepping for a big test, or staring down a monster project, keep these strategies in your back pocket.

Fact or fiction: can a growth mindset boost your grades?

Spoiler alert: it's not fiction. Let's dive into the real deal.

What if we told you that simply believing in your ability to grow and learn could help you do better in school? Sounds like magic, right? But it's not. It's all about having a "growth mindset."

The Program for International Student Assessment (PISA) ran a massive study involving 600,000 teens from 78 countries. They found out that students who believed they could improve their own intelligence—those with a "growth mindset"—scored higher in all subjects compared to those who thought their smarts were set in stone. And it wasn't just a tiny difference. We're talking about scoring 31.5 points higher in reading, 27 points in science, and 23 points in math. That's no small change!

THE POWER OF **YET**: YOUR SECRET WEAPON IN SCHOOL

CHALLENGING CHEMISTRY ASSIGNMENT

DEMANDING GYM CLASS

DIFFICULT MATH PROBLEM

CONFUSING ESSAY TOPIC

YET

MASTERING NEW DANCE MOVES

SUCCESS!

Girls, in particular, seemed to get an extra academic boost from having a strong growth mindset. And here's an interesting tidbit: different countries had different levels of growth mindset vibes. For example, a whopping 75% of students in Estonia, Denmark, and Germany demonstrated a growth mindset, and they happened to perform really well on PISA tests.

IT'S SCIENCE!

But that's not all. You know how some teachers just get you? They're there to help, they adapt to your learning style, and they give you meaningful feedback. Those teacher practices can actually help build a growth mindset in students.

And guess what? Students who had these supportive teachers were 4 percentage points more likely to have a growth mindset. In the United States, if you have a growth mindset and a supportive teacher, you could outscore your fixed mindset peers by 72 points in reading. Yes, you read that right!

Carol Dweck, the psychologist behind the growth mindset theory, says it's about more than just believing you can grow. **It's about creating a classroom environment that's like a petri dish for a growth mindset, where everyone values understanding, progress, and learning from mistakes.**

It's not just about studying harder or smarter. It's about believing in yourself and having the right environment to support your growth. Now, that's some food for thought!

Mindset makeover: transitioning from a fixed to growth mindset

If you're reading this, it means you're all set to transform the way you think—from a fixed to a growth mindset. I can already hear you saying, "that sounds awesome but...how exactly do I do it?" No worries, you're in the right section. Here, we're going to break down the steps. But remember, this change won't happen in the blink of an eye. It's more like learning to ride a bike for the first time; it needs practice and patience.

Step 1: Become a detective...of your thoughts

What's the first step? Paying attention to your thoughts. Be on the lookout for those sneaky fixed mindset thoughts like "I can't do this" or "this is beyond me." They're the little gremlins we need to expose!

Step 2: Question those thoughts

Caught a gremlin? Great! Now question it. "Is this actually true, or have I just not figured it out yet?" Remember, your brain is built to learn and adapt.

Step 3: Opt for growth

Alright, time to switch things up. Replace "I can't do this" with "I can't do this... yet." Just one little word, but oh boy, does it pack a punch! It's like unlocking a door to a world full of possibilities.

Step 4: Face your challenges, with confidence!

Here's where you get into the game. Face your challenges, and when you trip up (you will, it's part of the process), view it as a bonus level, a chance to learn something new.

Step 5: Become your own coach

After taking action, take a moment to reflect. What worked out for you? What didn't? What might you change for the next round? This reflection stage is your power-up station, where you refuel and prepare for your next challenge.

Now let's take a look at the growth mindset in action and learn from someone who's walked the talk!

Okay, so let's take a tour through the life of this really cool person—Danica McKellar. Does Winnie Cooper from the classic TV show "The Wonder Years" ring a bell? Yep, that's her. But here's the twist— she's not just a TV star. She's a legit math whiz, too! But trust me, she didn't wake up one day with mad math skills.

So here's the scoop: there was a time when math and Danica were like cats and dogs. She'd tell herself that she just wasn't a "math person."

But then, something clicked. She started spotting those sneaky fixed mindset thoughts and kicked them to the curb. Instead of thinking, "I'm a disaster at math," she switched it up to: "I haven't nailed math... yet." She jumped into her math homework, got help when she hit a wall and didn't let tough problems ruin her day.

Do you want to know what happened next? Over time, math changed from her nemesis to her buddy. Kind of like a challenging puzzle game she couldn't wait to beat. Her grades started going up, but the real win was that she actually started having fun wrestling with those math problems. She showed herself that she could crush something she once feared.

Here's the coolest part: Danica was so inspired by her own journey, she wrote a series of bestselling math books just for middle-school girls. She wanted to show them that they could kick their math fears to the curb, too.

So, are you game to switch things up like Danica? Yeah, it might feel like a rocky ride sometimes, but that's part of the thrill. The key is to keep on keeping on, never stop learning, and continue to grow. Trust me, you've got more potential than you think!

So, don't back down. Keep working that brain. Keep pushing past your limits. Keep growing. Because with a growth mindset, every hurdle is a stepping stone, every setback is a lesson, and every effort brings you closer to your dreams. You're just getting started—remember, the future is all about growth!

CHAPTER 6

Building Stronger Relationships With a Growth Mindset

So we've been talking a lot about the growth mindset, right? About how it's all about being open to learning, improving, and, yep, even failing. Well, guess what? It's not just about school or personal growth. This magical thing called the 'growth mindset' plays a significant part in our relationship dynamics too.

'Wait, what?', You may think. 'Relationship dynamics?' Is that another buzzword from those psychology books?

Alright, let me break it down for you. When we say 'relationship dynamics,' we're talking about the patterns or regular ways we interact and communicate with the people in our lives. Think of it like a dance between two people. Sometimes you lead, sometimes you follow, and sometimes you both improvise. The way this dance unfolds, that's the relationship dynamic.

The growth mindset dance

But here's the thing. When you put on the 'growth mindset' dancing shoes, your dance changes. Instead of stubbornly leading or passively following, you're ready to learn new moves, try different rhythms, or even switch roles.

That's what a growth mindset brings to the party of relationships: a curiosity and willingness to evolve together. To make this even clearer, it's like this: a fixed mindset would say, "this is how I am, take it or leave it," but a growth mindset

answers, "this is how I am now, but I'm open to growing and improving for the betterment of our relationship."

And guess what? This mindset can make a massive difference in how we connect with friends, family, or even that special someone. So, are you ready to dance?

Friendships & family: growth mindset at play

This whole growth mindset thing is not an individual sport but a team game, especially when we're talking about relationships. And no, we're not just talking about your bestie or your little brother, but all the people you hang around with—friends, family, even the people you bump into every day.

Imagine this: instead of holding a grudge because your sibling borrowed your favorite hoodie without asking (again!), You could use this situation as a growth opportunity. Sounds weird, right? But think about it: maybe it's a chance for you to express your boundaries better or find a creative solution.

And remember the friend who never texts back on time? Instead of labeling them as 'careless' or 'forgetful', you could choose to see this as an opportunity to understand their world better. Maybe they are just bad at time management, or they are juggling more responsibilities than you thought. This understanding doesn't excuse their behavior but encourages a conversation, a chance to improve your friendship.

Jake's journey from outsider to statistician
Once upon a time, Jake was just a kid who felt out of place among his friends. He wasn't a huge sports fan and often felt like the odd one out in a group that loved to talk about the latest games. While his friends bonded over their favorite teams and players, Jake struggled to share the same enthusiasm. He felt left out, disconnected, and a bit 'awkward.'

Then, Jake discovered the idea of a growth mindset, and it was a total game-changer for him. Instead of feeling isolated, he decided to use this as an opportunity to learn about sports from a different perspective. Instead of focusing on the gameplay, he dove into the numbers behind it all, the stats, the odds, the analytics.

And guess what happened? He fell in love with it. The statistics of sports, something most people found dry and boring, were exciting to Jake. He found his unique niche in the world of sports, one that not only allowed him to connect with his friends but also showcased his strengths.

Soon, Jake became the one his friends turned to for match predictions. His unique perspective on sports, combined with his knack for number crunching, made him an invaluable part of the group. He felt more connected to his friends than ever before, all because he decided to approach his situation with a growth mindset.

See, Jake's story isn't about magical powers or superhero strengths. It's about an everyday kid who chose to look at things differently. He decided to learn and grow, transforming his feelings of isolation into a path that eventually could lead him to become a world-renowned statistician.

So, if you ever feel 'different' or 'out of place,' remember Jake's story. Embrace your unique self, cultivate a growth mindset, and see where your journey takes you. Who knows, you might just discover your own unique passion and strength!

Emotional intelligence: the art of understanding and managing emotions

Hold up, we're about to get real about emotions. Ever wonder how some folks seem to just "get" other people? They're the ones who know exactly what to say when a friend's feeling blue. It's like they have a sixth sense for feelings. Well, you guessed it—that's emotional intelligence.

Emotional intelligence is your ninja skill for understanding, handling, and expressing your emotions positively and supporting others to do the same. It can help you talk things out better, handle conflict like a pro, and boost your relationships. Now, don't you want that ninja skill in your toolkit?

Mapping your emotions

Now that we know what emotional intelligence is, let's get into the 'how.' How do you acknowledge and manage your emotions, especially when things go sideways?

First things first, it's totally cool to have emotions. All of them—even the ones that feel like a storm in the middle of your sunshine. The secret isn't to push them away but to get to know them. Think of your feelings as messengers. They've got something important to say. Maybe you're peeved because that math test didn't go well, or you're buzzing with joy because your crush sent you a dm first. Whatever the message, it's key to listen and figure out what your emotions are saying.

Next up, once you've acknowledged your emotions, it's time to manage them. **And just to be clear, managing isn't about suppressing.** It's about finding ways to express your feelings that are good for you. Maybe that's taking a few deep breaths when your little brother is driving you nuts or jotting down your thoughts in a journal when things feel too much.

And here's the thing, it's all good if you don't get it right away. Mastering your emotions is kind of like getting good at skateboarding or nailing that new video game level. You won't ace it straight away. It takes practice and a whole lot of patience, and that's all part of the process. Each step, no matter how small, is progress toward becoming emotionally intelligent.

So, are you game for this emotional intelligence ride? It might be a bit bumpy at times, but the pay-off? Totally worth it. It's your golden ticket to relationships that are stronger, healthier, and more meaningful. Trust me, this is one adventure you'll want to sign up for!

Empathy and conflict resolution: walking in their shoes

Have you ever thought about what it feels like to step into someone else's shoes? Not literally, of course, but in a mental and emotional sense. That's what empathy is all about.

Empathy is like having a secret key that unlocks a deeper understanding of the people around you. It's about really "getting" where they're coming from. And you know what? That's incredibly valuable in friendships and family relationships. Do you know why? Because understanding leads to more patience, less quick judgment, and way more chill conversations.

For example, think about that moment when your friend forgets to return your call. You might be tempted to feel a bit ignored. But, when you remember that they've been dealing with a lot of homework and family stuff lately, you get where they're coming from. And just like that, you're not upset anymore. That, my friend, is empathy doing its magic.

Conflict resolution: The growth mindset way

Let's be real, no one likes disagreements. They're like an annoying fly that you just can't seem to swat away. But did you know a growth mindset could be your very own fly swatter?

When we talk about a "growth mindset," we're referring to the idea of seeing challenges as chances to learn and grow, rather than just irritating obstacles. In disagreements, this means realizing that a little spat isn't the end of the world. In fact, it might just be the start of understanding each other better, learning more about yourself, and making your relationships even stronger.

For instance, imagine you're squabbling with your sibling about who gets to hog the TV remote. Now, you could just storm off, or you could see it as an opportunity for growth. You could propose to create a TV schedule, or take turns, or even better, discover a new show that both of you love!

See, a growth mindset shows you that a compromise isn't losing. It's about getting the other person's perspective and coming up with a solution that

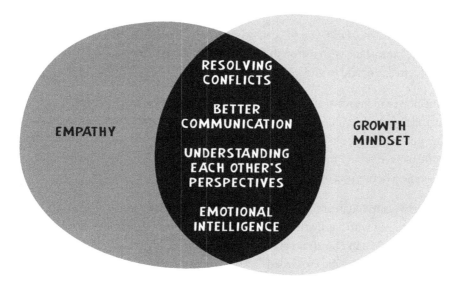

EMPATHY + GROWTH MINDSET = STRONGER RELATIONSHIPS

doesn't leave anyone feeling left out. So, the next time you're in the middle of a disagreement, try on your growth mindset cap. You might just be surprised by how much it changes the game.

With a sprinkle of empathy and a dash of growth mindset, you're armed and ready to navigate the maze of relationships. Go ahead, dive in, and make every interaction a memorable one!

A real-life relationship transformation

Maria and her older sister used to argue all the time, about who got the bathroom first in the morning to whose turn it was to do the dishes. The constant bickering was draining, and their relationship was on rocky ground.

Then Maria discovered the concept of the growth mindset in a school workshop. It was a light bulb moment for her. She realized that the fights with her sister weren't just about the bathroom or dishes. They were about understanding, patience, and compromise.

So, Maria made a conscious effort to empathize more with her sister, to understand her perspective, and find common ground. It wasn't smooth sailing, but with each disagreement, Maria chose to learn and grow rather than hold a grudge. Over time, the constant fights reduced, and Maria and her sister started understanding each other better.

Remember, like Maria, you too can bring about a positive transformation in your relationships with a growth mindset. All it takes is a willingness to understand, to learn, and to grow. You've got this!

The power to improve and strengthen your relationships lies in your hands. It's all about understanding that challenges, misunderstandings, and conflicts are not stumbling blocks. They're not things that make you say, "ugh, this is so difficult. I'm done." Instead, they're opportunities for you to grow, learn, and become a better person.

It might seem tough at first. And that's okay. Change isn't always a walk in the park. But with a growth mindset, even the steepest mountain becomes climbable. So don't be afraid of those tricky spots in your relationships. They're not dead ends. They're crossroads where you can decide to take the route that leads to growth and understanding.

And remember, you're not alone in this journey. If things get tough, don't hesitate to reach out. Talk to a friend, a family member, a mentor, or a counselor. Sharing your experiences and thoughts can help you gain new perspectives and insights.

Here's to you and your journey toward healthier, happier relationships. Keep growing!

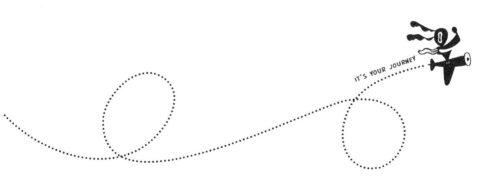

IT'S YOUR JOURNEY

Growing by sharing your thoughts?

We're super excited that you're on this growth mindset journey with *The Essential Growth Mindset Handbook for Teens*. We hope you've already started seeing the power of "yet," and you're finding ways to embrace failures as lessons. If you've found the insights helpful so far, we'd love to hear your thoughts!

Remember the power of "yet"? Just like how it's applied to learning and growing, it's applicable here too! Maybe you haven't written a book review... yet. But here's a great opportunity to take that leap and grow. It only takes a minute, and your feedback can inspire so many others to start adopting a growth mindset.

Your words matter—a lot! Your insights not only help us improve, but they also guide future readers who are just starting on their growth mindset journey. Plus, writing that review? That's a mini victory to celebrate!

So, thank you for stepping up and giving this growth thing a go. We're really looking forward to hearing what you think!

Scan this QR code to leave a quick 1-minute review!

Your input helps us all grow, not just you and us, but also other teens, parents, and educators looking for guidance on fostering a growth mindset. Sharing your thoughts is like passing the baton in this exciting relay of personal growth.

We appreciate you joining this community of growth mindset champions. And we're thrilled to explore the next part of the journey. Ready to uncover more about how the growth mindset can transform your daily life? Let's keep going!

CHAPTER 7

Growth Mindset in Sport and Extra-curricular activities

Right now, we're stepping into the world of sports, hobbies, and all those fun activities you fill your free time with. You know, the stuff that makes you forget about homework and that history test coming up next week. But what if I told you that there's a secret sauce, a game-changer, that could amp up your enjoyment and performance in these activities? That's where the growth mindset comes into play.

Let's hit pause for a moment and think about it. Have you ever found yourself stuck in the middle of a tough game or a tricky piano piece, thinking, "I'll never get this right"? Yeah, we've all been there. This is where our mental game steps in. The way we think about ourselves and our abilities has a massive impact on how we tackle challenges and setbacks in sports and extracurricular activities.

You see, with a fixed mindset, you might believe that your abilities are, well, fixed. That can be a downer, right? But with a growth mindset, you'll see every missed goal or muffed note as an opportunity to learn and grow. Yeah, that sounds a lot better, doesn't it?

Our goal in this chapter is to make this growth mindset stuff as real to you as that football you kick around, that paintbrush you masterfully wield, or that guitar you're learning to play. We want to show you how this whole growth mindset gig isn't just for the classroom. It can level up your game in sports and other activities, making them even more enjoyable and rewarding.

So, why is this growth mindset thing such a crucial component for your hobbies and sports, you might ask? Well, it supercharges your abilities, not by magically making you better overnight (we wish, right?), But by giving you the mental tools to push through challenges, learn from mistakes, and ultimately become the best version of you.

This chapter is all about turning you into a mindset master in the realm of sports and extracurriculars. It's about showing you how you can use this game-changing growth mindset to elevate your game and have even more fun while doing it. Let's score some mindset goals together!

The performance boost: level up with growth mindset

Imagine you're playing your favorite video game. You're all in, eyes glued to the screen, heart racing, hands a little sweaty. The game gets challenging, but you keep at it because you're hooked, and it's just too much fun. Now, wouldn't it be fantastic if you could bring that same energy and determination to your sports or extracurricular activities?

Good news! A growth mindset is like a cheat code for your performance in real life. It's not going to give you superhuman strength or the ability to fly (how awesome would that be, though?), But it will help you push your limits, overcome obstacles, and enjoy the journey. The idea here is pretty simple: believing that you can improve and learn from your mistakes can seriously enhance your performance and make the whole process more enjoyable.

It's not just about performing better, though. It's also about enjoying the process. Picture this: you're playing a basketball game. If you're all stressed out about whether you'll win or lose, you're probably not having much fun. But if you switch your focus to learning and growing, to getting better with each pass and shot, suddenly the whole game becomes a lot more fun.

And it's not just for sports! Maybe you're part of a drama club, a band, or a chess club. In all these activities, having a growth mindset can make a big difference. Let's say you're learning to play a new piece on the piano. Instead

of getting frustrated with each wrong note, you could look at each mistake as a chance to improve, to figure out the right chords and rhythm. Suddenly, practicing that difficult piece becomes less of a chore and more of a challenge, something to look forward to.

So, whether you're shooting hoops, painting a portrait, or strumming a guitar, remember that your mindset is like a secret power. When you face a challenge, don't stress. Just remember: you're learning, you're growing, and most importantly, you're becoming even better than you already are.

Powering through: riding the waves with a growth mindset

We've all had moments when things didn't go as planned. You didn't make the cut for the basketball team. Your band's performance was less than stellar. That new painting technique you were trying out? Not as instagram-worthy as you thought. Bummer, right? Well, what if I told you that there's a way to power through these hiccups, and come out stronger on the other side?

When you trip and stumble, it can be tempting to wallow in self-pity and think "I'm just not good enough." But hang on! That's the fixed mindset speaking. And we're all about growth here, aren't we? A growth mindset tells you "I may have stumbled now, but that doesn't define me. I can get better."

Let's say you didn't make the cut for the basketball team. A fixed mindset might tell you to give up, that basketball isn't for you. But with a growth mindset, you could see this as a chance to figure out what went wrong. Maybe you need to work on your three-pointers or your defense game. Identify the problem areas, work on them, and who knows? You could be the star player next season!

Here are some tips on how to cultivate this attitude.

- First, **don't be afraid of criticism.** Instead, see it as constructive feedback. If your band's performance didn't go well, don't blame it on the acoustics or the audience. Listen to the feedback, figure out where you went wrong, and use it to improve for next time.

- Second, **remember that it's okay to ask for help.** Nobody becomes a pro overnight. If you're struggling with a painting technique, maybe you can ask your art teacher for some extra guidance. Or watch tutorials, or read up on it. There's no shame in needing help. It's actually a sign of strength and a big step towards improvement.

- Third, **try to focus on the process, not just the outcome.** Sure, winning feels great, but getting better is just as important, if not more. Celebrate the small victories. Did you nail that tricky guitar riff today, even if it was just once? That's progress, my friend!

Setbacks can feel like mountains, but remember, even the most challenging peaks are climbed one step at a time. With a growth mindset, you're not just equipped to climb, you're ready to conquer. So go ahead, power through those setbacks, and watch as they turn into comebacks!

Under pressure: unleashing your inner cool with a growth mindset

Here's the thing about stress and pressure—they're everywhere. Whether you're stepping onto the basketball court, preparing to showcase your acting skills on stage, or even trying out for the school debate team, it's natural to feel butterflies in your stomach. But hey, feeling pressure isn't always a bad thing. It means you're stepping out of your comfort zone and challenging yourself. And that's where a growth mindset comes into play.

Ever noticed how some people just seem to thrive under pressure, while others, well, not so much? That's often the difference between a fixed mindset and a growth mindset. If you believe your abilities are set in stone (that's the fixed mindset, remember?), Then stress can become your worst enemy. It can make you freeze, stumble, and even give up.

But when you believe you can improve (hello, growth mindset!), The pressure turns into an exciting challenge. A bump on the road? Bring it on! Now, I'm not saying you'll start loving pressure instantly, but here are some strategies to help you handle it like a champ.

- **First off, remember, pressure is not a reflection of your worth.** Flubbed a line during the school play? That doesn't mean you're a bad actor. It means there's room for growth. Accept that mistakes happen and focus on learning from them instead of beating yourself up.

- **Secondly, embrace the journey.** Instead of focusing solely on the outcome, like whether you'll win the match or not, why not cherish the whole journey? Appreciate the practice sessions, the team camaraderie, and the skills you're developing along the way. When you learn to value the process over the final result, pressure tends to take a backseat.

- **Finally, practice mindfulness.** When you feel the pressure creeping up on you, take a moment to breathe. Mindfulness can help you stay focused, keep your emotions in check, and ultimately perform better. Whether it's through meditation, journaling, or just taking a quiet walk, find a mindfulness practice that works for you. (Make sure to turn to Chapter 9 for some practical and simple mindfulness tips and tricks).

So next time you're under pressure, remember—it's not a monster waiting to get you. It's an opportunity for growth. A chance to challenge yourself and become better. With a growth mindset, you're not just surviving under pressure—you're thriving. And who knows, you might just find that pressure can be the key to unlocking your full potential!

Growth mindset spotlight: the tale of the GOAT

Let's talk about a legend whose journey personifies the power of a growth mindset. That's right, we're talking about the undeterred master of the court— Serena Williams!

Serena's journey began not in a plush tennis academy, but on the public courts of Compton, California. As a young girl, she faced a myriad of obstacles but her belief and relentless drive propelled her forward.

The road to stardom wasn't smooth for Serena. She experienced her first major setback at the tender age of 14 when age-eligibility restrictions denied her a wild-card entry to make her professional debut in the Bank of the West Classic. But she didn't let this setback slow her down. She viewed it as an opportunity to learn and grow, a stepping stone toward her future success.

Between 2004 and 2006, persistent knee injuries took a toll on Serena's performance. In 2004, a left knee injury kept her off the court until the Miami open. The following year, she started strong with a win in Melbourne, only to face another setback—an ankle injury that forced her to skip the French Open. This led to her finishing the year outside the top 10 for the first time. Despite limited play in 2006 due to continued knee issues, she never lost her spirit.

Serena's battles weren't limited to injuries. In 2011, she faced a life-threatening situation—a hematoma and a pulmonary embolism. But with characteristic resilience, she bounced back, starting her season midway from the grass-court part of the season.

More setbacks came her way in 2016 when she had to withdraw from the Hopman Cup due to knee inflammation, and later, she had to pull out of the Rogers Cup due to shoulder inflammation.

Most recently, in 2020, Serena had to call an early end to her season due to an achilles tendon injury, which was a massive blow to her. Despite all these hurdles, Serena remained steadfast, and it was her growth mindset that led her to retake the world no.1 Singles ranking, turning each setback into a comeback.

Serena once said, **"I really think a champion is defined not by their wins but by how they can recover when they fall."** This statement perfectly encapsulates her unwavering growth mindset. She saw every setback not as a failure, but as an opportunity to grow.

The power of growth mindset
Today, Serena's name is synonymous with greatness. She holds an awe-inspiring 23 Grand Slam singles titles and continues to inspire millions worldwide.

But the true lesson of Serena's story isn't about the glitter of trophies or the charm of fame. It's about her journey, her resilience, and her refusal to be defined by her losses. It's about an unwavering belief in her ability to grow, adapt, and improve. It's a testament to how a growth mindset can transform obstacles into stepping stones, and dreams into reality.

So remember, a growth mindset isn't exclusive to tennis legends—it's a tool for us all. The next time you face a challenge, think of Serena. Embrace it, learn from it, and continue to grow. That's the real secret to mastering this game called life!

Practical tips: your growth mindset playbook

Now, let's bring it all home and see how you can sprinkle some growth mindset magic on your own sports, hobbies, or extracurricular activities.

Tip 1: Redefine winning

Let's say you're a basketball player. Instead of defining "winning" as scoring the most points, redefine it as making the most of each play, improving your skills, or even helping your teammates shine. Yeah, keeping score is part of the game. But what if you started keeping score of how much you learned and improved instead?

Tip 2: Meet setbacks with a high-five

Imagine you're in the drama club, and you totally forgot your lines during a performance. Major facepalm, right? Not so fast! Instead of beating yourself up, high-five that setback and say, "thanks for the lesson!" It's a chance to work harder on memorization, or maybe it's a sign you were super nervous and need to work on calming your stage fright. Every setback is a set-up for a comeback, remember?

Tip 3: Embrace the challenge

You're on the chess team, and you're about to face the top-ranked player in the tournament. Your stomach is doing somersaults. But instead of running for the hills, you tell yourself, "this is a fantastic opportunity to grow!" Embrace the challenge, and no matter the outcome, you come out stronger and smarter.

Tip 4: Celebrate growth in others

Maybe you're on the debate team, and one of your teammates just made a killer argument. Instead of feeling envious or threatened, celebrate their growth! Remember, a rising tide lifts all boats. When one of us gets better, we all get better.

By taking these tips and painting them over your own activities, you'll start to see a shift. It might not happen overnight, but that's okay. A growth mindset is all about, well, growth! And growth takes time. You might stumble along the way, and that's okay, too. Remember, it's not about being perfect. It's about getting a little bit better each time.

So, next time you step onto the field, onto the stage, or into the club meeting, take a deep breath and remember: a growth mindset isn't just about winning or losing, it's about learning, growing, and most importantly, enjoying the ride. And who knows? You might just surprise yourself with how far you can go!

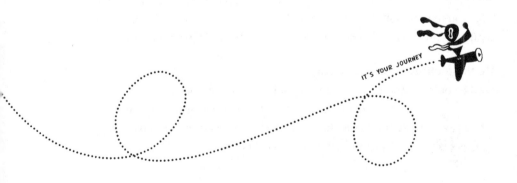

IT'S YOUR JOURNEY

CHAPTER 8

Turning Growth Mindset into Action— the Art of Effective Goal Setting

Now, we're going to talk about something that's not just about scoring the winning goal or hitting the high note in the choir—we're going to talk about goals. Yes, your personal goals: your academic aspirations, self-improvement challenges, fitness milestones, and every single victory in between.

Remember that sense of achievement when you nailed that complex skateboard trick after countless tries? Or when you cracked that difficult math problem and aced the test? That's the power of goal-setting in action. Goals, whether big or small, act as our guiding stars, keeping us focused, and driving us in the right direction. And the thrill of accomplishing them? It's unbeatable!

So, why all the fuss about goal-setting? Because it's incredibly important, especially for you, the next-gen leaders. Goals are not just meant for adults pursuing career milestones or marathon runs. They are our individual roadmap to success and fulfillment. They help us identify our desires, ambitions and set us on a path to achieve them.

Setting goals is like signing up for a mission. It's not aimless wandering but a purposeful journey with a clear destination in sight. This sense of direction fuels our motivation, adds an exciting dimension to everyday life, and, most importantly, aids in fostering a growth mindset.

Here's the connection: embracing a growth mindset is about believing in your capacity to learn, grow, and improve. Similarly, goal setting is about taking that belief and turning it into action. It provides a platform for growth, offering opportunities to experience challenges, overcome obstacles, and savor victories.

The thrill of the journey towards these goals, with all its unpredictable twists and turns, highs and lows, can be as rewarding as achieving the goal itself. It's an epic adventure, filled with abundant learning opportunities.

However, not all goals are created equal. Some are specific and precise, like reading 50 books in a year, while others are vague and broad, like 'being more creative' or 'doing well in school.' While there's nothing inherently wrong with the latter, they lack a clear pathway to success.

This is where the art of effective goal-setting steps in, and trust me, it's a game-changer. It's about setting clear, actionable, and measurable goals. This approach, combined with a growth mindset, serves as your personalized success navigator. Remember, the journey can be just as exhilarating, enlightening, and fulfilling as reaching your destination.

The SMART way: effective goal setting

So, remember when we said setting clear and meaningful goals is super important? That's where the SMART way of goal-setting swoops in. Now, don't get all, "oh, another acronym? Really?" This one is a total game-changer and if you've read any of our previous books, I'm sure you're familiar! And yes, it's as smart as it sounds. SMART stands for Specific, Measurable, Achievable, Relevant, and Time-bound. Let's break this down:

S: Specific

We start with "Specific." The 'S' in SMART. So, instead of setting a goal like "I want to get better at guitar," you could say, "I want to learn how to play 'stairway to heaven' on the guitar." See the difference? The second goal gives you a clear target. It's not just about being better; it's about conquering that epic Led Zeppelin masterpiece.

M: Measurable

Next up is "Measurable," our 'M.' Let's take a fitness goal, for instance. Instead of just saying "I want to get stronger," make it measurable: "I want to be able to do 50 push-ups non-stop." That's something you can track and measure. You know exactly when you've hit your target, and that's way more satisfying.

A: Achievable

The 'A' in smart stands for "Achievable." Now, we're all for dreaming big, but setting realistic goals is key. Wanting to be a millionaire by next week? Probably not achievable (unless you're planning to win the lottery!). But saving up enough money for that new gaming console by doing extra chores? Now we're talking!

R: Relevant

Our 'R' stands for "Relevant." Your goals should matter to you and align with your bigger life objectives. If you're really into art and want to enhance your skills, setting a goal to master the piano might not be as relevant as, say, learning a new painting technique.

T: Time-bound

Last but definitely not least, 'T' is for "Time-bound." Deadlines aren't just for homework assignments, they're super helpful for our goals too. Giving yourself a timeframe keeps the pressure on (in a good way!). So, instead of saying "I want to read more books," try "I want to read one book per month."

The SMART way to set goals might seem like a bit of work initially, but once you get the hang of it, you'll see how much easier it makes achieving your goals. Remember, a well-defined goal is like a lighthouse guiding your way. And with the SMART technique, you've got one powerful lighthouse on your side!

Ready to give it a shot? Let's move on and see how a growth mindset ties into all of this!

Growth mindset and goals: the power combo

Alright, so you've got your SMART goals on the ready. But what if I told you there's another secret ingredient that can supercharge your goal-setting strategy? Let's dive into the dynamic duo of growth mindset and goal setting!

Growth mindset and goal setting: the perfect pair

Imagine you're on your way towards a goal, and suddenly you hit a major obstacle. If you're hanging out with the fixed mindset crew, you might be tempted to throw in the towel, believing you just don't have what it takes. But, if you're part of the growth mindset squad, you'd view this obstacle as a learning opportunity. It's not a roadblock, but a stepping stone, a chance to try something new, and develop yourself. You'd say, "alright, plan A didn't work, but the alphabet has 25 more letters!" Now, doesn't that feel more empowering?

Supercharging your success trifecta: motivation, resilience, and adaptability

Having a growth mindset doesn't just make you an optimist, though. It also gives a solid boost to your motivation, resilience, and adaptability, a trio that's absolutely vital for achieving your goals.

Think of it this way. Your goal is a destination, discipline is the car that drives you there, resilience is the fuel that keeps the car running, and adaptability is your GPS that reroutes when you hit a dead end.

For example, let's say you're trying to become a chess whiz. Your discipline gets you to sit down every day for a practice session. But you're bound to face setbacks, like losing a match or not being able to figure out a certain strategy. With a growth mindset, though, you wouldn't let that dampen your spirits. You'd bounce back (hey there, resilience!) And try different strategies (nice to see you, adaptability!). Bit by bit, you'll see yourself improving, and that's the power of a growth mindset!

 So, when it comes to setting and working towards your goals, a growth mindset can be a real game-changer.

Hands-on help: worksheets and exercises

Alright! Enough chit-chat about theory, right? Let's jump into some real-world, practical stuff. We've got some goal-setting templates and activities to make things visual and applicable, help you stick to your goals, and check on your progress regularly. These will not only help you set your smart goals but also give you some cool tips on growing that awesome trait called resilience.

Goal setting: your personal blueprint

First things first, we've included a handy smart goal-setting worksheet at the end of this book in the Resources section (or if you're reading our ebook click here to download it directly). Feel free to use it as many times as you'd like no matter how big or small your goal.

This template is purposefully built to walk you through the process of setting your own effective smart goals, focusing on each component one step at a time.

Think of this worksheet as your personal goal-setting buddy. It's there to guide you in setting and chasing after your objectives, whether it's to be the MVP of your basketball team or to ace your computer programming course. The magic of this template is in how it breaks down your goal into manageable, concrete steps.

Here's a quick run-through of how you might use it:

1. **Specific:** you'll start by clearly defining what you want to achieve. No vague ambitions here!

2. **Measurable:** next, you'll detail how you'll track your progress. Maybe it's the number of baskets you make during practice or the scores on your coding assignments.

3. **Achievable:** after that, you'll confirm that your goal is within your reach. It's cool to aim high, but make sure it's something you can realistically work towards.

4. **Relevant:** then, you'll check that your goal aligns with your larger life plans. If you dream of being a video game designer, that coding course suddenly becomes super relevant, right?

5. **Time-bound:** lastly, you'll set a deadline. Having a clear end date helps keep the pressure on (in a good way) and prevents your goal from turning into a 'someday' kind of thing.

The aim isn't to rush to the finish line but to consistently make progress and that's where this tracker can come in handy. It's all about growing, not being flawless.

Stay tuned for the growth mindset exercises in the 50-day growth mindset challenge!

In our 50-day growth mindset challenge (in Chapter 10), we have activities geared towards growing your resilience and flexing that growth mindset of yours. These are all about helping you develop your bounce-back ability when faced with challenges.

Our favorite activity is the "flip the script" exercise (on day 23!). You start by writing down a challenge you've faced recently. Then, you brainstorm ways you can flip that into an opportunity for learning. Trust us, this exercise can be a total game-changer.

 We also have several activities that are all about learning from setbacks. Because hey, setbacks are a part of life, right? But with a growth mindset, you can learn to see them as stepping stones, not stumbling blocks.

Remember, take your time with them, ponder over your responses, and most importantly, enjoy the process. Remember, you're not just filling out work-sheets—you're laying the groundwork for your future success. So, let's roll up those sleeves and get down to it!

Your goals matter

We want you to understand that your goals matter. Big or small, they're yours, and they are important. Whether you're aiming to make the school basketball team or striving to learn a new language, your goal is your own personal finish line.

Working towards your goals gives you something to aim for. It fuels your determination, drives your motivation, and gives you a reason to push yourself out of your comfort zone. And it's the process of trying to get there that matters the most. It's about the journey, not just the destination.

Couple this goal-setting framework with a growth mindset and you'll learn to relish the process, accept setbacks as part of the path, and continually seek ways to grow.

CHAPTER 9

Embracing Growth Mindset for Stronger Mental Health and Well-being

L et's kick off a conversation on something we don't chat about enough—mental health and well-being. It's not all about avoiding the blues or stress. It's more like feeling comfortable in your own skin, handling the ups and downs, and creating a sense of balance in your life. Pretty important stuff, right?

First things first. We're going to break down these fancy terms—mental health and well-being. They're not just terms psychologists toss around, they're about you. Just like keeping your body healthy and strong, your mind needs its own kind of attention to stay fit.

 Think about all the stuff you're juggling. School, homework, sports, maybe a part-time job, family obligations, and attempting to have a social life squeezed in between. It's like spinning plates sometimes, and that's okay to acknowledge.

But we're not here to just nod at the issue. We're here to work on solutions too. One major game-changer is prioritizing your mental health. With a strong mental game, you're better equipped to tackle stress, make positive decisions, and feel good about yourself.

And here's the secret sauce—a growth mindset can play a huge part in promoting mental health. You know the drill, it's all about the belief that effort equals improvement. And just like it can help you score that goal or level up in your favorite game, a growth mindset can help you navigate through stress and bounce back stronger.

But don't just believe what we're saying. We're going to dig into what the experts have found about the connection between mental health and a growth mindset, and how you can use this info to manage stress and anxiety in your life. So, are you pumped to get your mind game on point?

Growth mindset: your ally against stress, anxiety, and depression

Stress. Anxiety. Depression. These are heavy words that we often skirt around. They're like unwanted guests that seem to show up at the worst times. But what if I told you that understanding them could be the key to managing them? You wouldn't just turn your back on a tough boss you need to beat in a game, right? So let's not back down from understanding these tough parts of life either.

Stress, for instance, isn't always the villain. It's a natural response when we're under pressure. But too much stress? Yeah, that's not fun. Then we've got anxiety, which is like a worry-wart that won't quit. It's normal to feel anxious now and then, but when it starts feeling like you're living in a constant state of 'what ifs', that's when it can become a problem.

Depression, on the other hand, isn't just feeling down. It's like being stuck in a gloomy weather forecast that just won't let up. And it's okay to admit if you're dealing with this—many of us do at some point. The important thing is to reach out for help if you're feeling this way.

Now, where does our growth mindset fit into all this? Great question. So, you know how we talked about seeing challenges as opportunities for growth? That's the core of a growth mindset. It doesn't promise a life free from stress, anxiety, or depression. But it gives you a powerful tool to manage them.

Imagine stress as a huge wall blocking your path. With a growth mindset, you're not just looking at the wall and thinking it's too high to climb. Instead, you're thinking of ways to get around it, over it, or even through it.

There's some cool research that backs this up too. Studies show that people with a growth mindset are more likely to use positive coping strategies, like seeking support, problem-solving, and looking for the silver lining in tough situations. These are some solid tools to have in your mental health toolkit, right?

So, while it won't make stress, anxiety, or depression vanish into thin air, a growth mindset can definitely give you the strength to face them head-on. Kind of like a secret superpower, don't you think?

If you're looking for surefire ways to learn the keys to stress management (especially for teens in the 2020s), don't miss out on our book, *The Essential Stress Management Handbook for Teens.* Packed with timely and teen-focused solutions, it's your ultimate guide to mastering stress management in the 2020s and beyond.

Self-care isn't selfish: the need for relaxation and downtime

You know what's absolutely epic? You. Yeah, I said it. You're epic. You're like the protagonist in your very own adventure story. But even the mightiest heroes need to recharge their health bars once in a while, right? So let's talk about something super important: self-care.

Okay, quick reality check: self-care isn't about always being in "treat yourself" mode. It's not all spa days and ice cream (though those are pretty awesome, too). Self-care is about doing stuff that keeps you feeling balanced and healthy. It's about making choices that respect your mental, emotional, and physical health. So yeah, it's a pretty big deal.

A growth mindset comes in clutch when it comes to self-care. Why? Well, self-care sometimes means doing things that aren't super exciting in the moment. Like getting a good night's sleep instead of binge-watching your favorite show until 3 am. Or choosing to go for a run when you'd rather veg out on the couch. A growth mindset helps us see the value in these choices, not as boring chores, but as steps towards becoming our best selves.

**SELF-CARE:
THE KEY TO
MENTAL
HEALTH**

SELF-CARE, YO!

SOCIAL CONNECTION

MINDFULNESS

HOBBIES

EXERCISE

HEALTHY EATING

SLEEP

There's no one-size-fits-all approach to self-care, and that's totally okay. It's about finding what works for you. Love music? Maybe playing your favorite tunes or learning a new instrument could be your go-to stress-busters. Into art? Sketching, painting, or even creating digital art could be your way to unwind.

For some, it might mean spending time in nature or practicing yoga. For others, it could be all about hanging out with friends, playing video games, reading books, or whatever else makes you feel good. The important thing is to create a routine that you enjoy and can stick to. Think of it as programming your daily happiness cheat code.

So, remember: taking time for self-care isn't selfish. It's essential. And with a growth mindset, you can make it a habit that not only helps you relax and recharge but also keeps you growing, evolving, and smashing those life goals.

Embracing stillness: mindfulness and meditation

Welcome to the chill zone. It's time to pump the brakes, unplug from the chaos, and float into a world of calm. Sounds dreamy, right? Yeah, we thought so too. But how do we make that dream a reality? The magic words are mindfulness and meditation.

First off, what's the deal with mindfulness? Picture this: you're chilling out, no worries about that math homework due tomorrow, not fussing over that funky text your BFF sent you. Just you, hanging out in the moment. That's mindfulness. It's about letting go of yesterday's drama and tomorrow's worry, and just living in the now.

Then we have meditation. It's kind of like the gym for your brain, except instead of lifting weights, you're lifting your thoughts, focusing on your breathing, and training your mind to chill out. Imagine being the boss of your thoughts, not the other way around.

Let's give it a try. Find a quiet spot, get cozy, and close your eyes. Focus on your breath. Inhale. Exhale. Feel the air in your lungs, and let everything else fade into the background. If your brain decides to throw a party and invite a bunch of random thoughts, just kindly show them the door and return your focus to your breath. Voila, you're meditating!

"But hey," you might say, "this isn't as breezy as I thought!" That's cool, too. This is where your growth mindset rolls in like a superstar. **You know that learning a new skill isn't about nailing it on the first try.** It's about sticking with it, knowing that every moment you dedicate brings you one step closer to mastering it.

Mindfulness and meditation aren't just trendy hashtags, they're valuable tools that can help you surf life's waves with style. So take the plunge, ride those waves, and remember: your growth mindset has got your back.

Hands-on help: mindfulness and meditation exercises

Mindfulness and meditation can sound a bit mysterious, huh? Like something out of an ancient story where you sit on a mountain peak, contemplating life. Well, surprise, it's not that intense! It's actually something you can do right in your bedroom, at a park, or even during lunch break at school. So, let's explore how to get started with these awesome, mind-calming techniques.

You don't need a monk's robe or mystical chants. All you need is a comfy spot and a bit of time. Meditation can be as simple as focusing on your breath.

Inhale... exhale... just pay attention to the air entering and leaving your body. Thoughts popping up? That's normal! Just notice them, then let them float away like clouds in the sky. Return to your breath. Do this for a few minutes each day, and bam, you're meditating!

Mindfulness is all about being in the present. Instead of being on auto-pilot, going through your day, mindfulness means paying attention to what's happening right now. The smell of fresh-cut grass? The warmth of the sun on your skin? The flavor explosion of your favorite ice cream? Yup, that's mindfulness!

But how does all this help with mental health and what's this got to do with the growth mindset? Good question! Well, imagine you're stressing over a math test. A fixed mindset might make you think, "I'm terrible at math. I'll never pass." But if you practice mindfulness, you can catch that thought, observe it without judgment, and let it pass without spiraling into anxiety. Then, a growth mindset steps in, reminding you that it's not about being a math genius right now. It's about learning and growing, even if it's challenging.

Now for some hands-on help. We've got cool rad mindfulness and meditation exercises lined up for you! Up first a chocolatey experience!

The Mindful Chocolate Experience

 Alright, folks! We're about to do something that combines two of the best things in life: mindfulness and chocolate. Sounds deliciously intriguing, right? Welcome to the Mindful Chocolate Experience!

Remember mindfulness is all about staying in the present moment, fully aware of your surroundings, sensations, and feelings. It's a fantastic tool to cultivate our mental health and wellbeing. Let's start our journey into mindfulness with something that's delightful and definitely not a chore—savoring a piece of chocolate.

Here are the steps:

Step 1: Grab a piece of chocolate.
The type doesn't matter; it could be milk, dark, or white chocolate. Just make sure it's something you'd enjoy eating!

Step 2: Become a chocolate detective.
Before you pop it into your mouth, examine it like you're Sherlock Holmes.

Look at its color, shape, and texture. Is it smooth or rough? Are there any patterns on it?

Step 3: Get touchy-feely.
Hold it in your hand. How does it feel? Is it hard, soft, cool, or warm?

Step 4: Be nosy (in a good way!)
Next, bring the chocolate to your nose. What does it smell like? Can you identify the rich cocoa scent or maybe some notes of vanilla, fruit, or nuts?

Step 5: Go ahead, take a bite... but don't swallow yet
Finally, take a bite but don't swallow immediately. Let it sit in your mouth. How does it feel against your tongue? Is it melting, crumbling, or popping? What are the flavors that you can taste?

Step 6: All good things must come to an end
When you're ready, swallow the chocolate. Pay attention to that feeling. Can you still taste it? Do you notice a change in your mood or emotions?

Remember, there's no right or wrong way to do this. **The whole point is to engage all your senses and immerse yourself in the experience.**

This challenge might sound a bit unusual, but it's a great way to practice mindfulness. Plus, you get to eat chocolate! How cool is that?

By taking the time to really appreciate the chocolate, you're not only sharpening your senses but also cultivating a deeper sense of appreciation and understanding of your experiences. And that, my friends, is a key ingredient in nurturing our mental health and wellbeing. So, let's make the most of every moment (and every piece of chocolate), shall we?

The body scan meditation
Alright folks, ready to dive into a meditation that's all about getting in touch with your body? Welcome to the body scan meditation!

It's all about learning to focus your mind, connect with your body, and cultivate an awareness of the present moment. This is an awesome tool to add to your mental health toolbox.

Here's the step-by-step guide:

Step 1: find a quiet place

To kick off, you need to find a calm, quiet spot where you won't be disturbed. Could be your bedroom, a cozy corner, or even a quiet park. Anywhere you feel relaxed and comfortable will work.

Step 2: get comfortable

Sit or lie down in a position that feels comfortable for you. Remember, this isn't a competition to see who can twist into the craziest yoga pose. It's about being comfy, so your mind isn't distracted by physical discomfort.

Step 3: close your eyes

Close your eyes and take a moment to settle in.  Notice how your body feels against the surface you're on. If you're sitting, feel your feet touching the ground.

Step 4: breathe

Focus on your breath. Don't try to change it, just notice it. Is it fast, slow, deep, shallow? Feel your chest and belly rise and fall with each breath.

Step 5: scan your body

Now, imagine a warm, soothing light slowly moving down from the top of your head to your toes. As it moves, pay attention to each part of your body. Do you feel any tension, discomfort, or maybe nothing at all? That's okay. The point is to just observe, without judgment.

Step 6: release tension

As you find areas of tension or discomfort, imagine the light soothing and releasing that tension. Visualize the tension melting away and leaving your body.

Step 7: reflect

Once the light has reached your toes, take a moment to reflect. How do you feel? Do you notice a difference from before the meditation?

It might take a bit of practice to really feel connected to your body, but keep at it. Remember, the goal here isn't to become a meditation guru. It's about carving out time for you and your well-being while learning a valuable tool to help manage stress and cultivate mindfulness. So, give it a go. Your brain and body will thank you!

Here's the thing about mental health—it's not a one-and-done type of deal. It's an ongoing process. Like keeping a garden, you need to tend to it regularly.

And just like a gardener uses different tools to maintain their green space, your growth mindset is a crucial tool for nurturing your mental garden. It's not some magic wand that makes all the stress, anxiety, or blues disappear. But it does change how you deal with these feelings. Instead of letting them control you, a growth mindset allows you to acknowledge these feelings, learn from them, and use them to grow stronger.

Life will throw curveballs. Tests will be tough, relationships will have ups and downs, and hey, adulting can be pretty overwhelming. But with a growth mindset, you're not just surviving all this, you're thriving through it. You're learning, growing, and becoming the best version of yourself.

So, what's next? Keep practicing what you've learned in this chapter. Try those meditation techniques, engage with mindfulness during your day, and make self-care a part of your routine. Got a bad grade? Failed at something? Remember, it's not the end of the world. It's an opportunity to learn and grow.

Keep growing, keep learning, and keep being awesome! This is your journey, and with your growth mindset, you're more than ready to rock it!

CHAPTER 10
The 50-Day Growth Mindset Challenge!

Are you revved up to embark on this 50-day voyage to nurture a growth mindset? This isn't just about absorbing knowledge; it's about translating it into action. Understanding the concept of a growth mindset is just the start; you need to embody it. And for that, we've tailored an exact plan!

So, what's the essence of this plan? Picture it as a mental fitness routine. Just like athletes condition their bodies, over the subsequent 50 days, you'll participate in activities, solve quizzes, and dive into self-assessments. All this is designed to stretch and fortify your growth mindset muscles.

Now, you might wonder, why 50 days? Well, science suggests that around this time frame, we start to form robust habits. By adhering to this program for 50 days, you're offering your brain a legitimate shot at making the growth mindset your go-to setting.

As you immerse yourself in the program, you might notice some activities seem familiar. Here's the logic: repetition is the backbone of skill-building. Each iteration of these activities is a brick in the edifice of your new growth mindset. The more you practice, the deeper this habit ingrains itself into your everyday life.

And hey, remember, this journey isn't about a sprint to the finish line. Rather, it's akin to a scenic trail hike where you pause, soak in the landscapes, take stock of your journey, and appreciate your progress. You might stumble, or even stray, but that's all part of this extraordinary growth adventure.

Each day, you'll delve into activities that will challenge you, provoke introspection, and maybe even surprise you. You'll explore your inner workings, unlock your potential, and learn how to morph setbacks into epic comebacks.

A virtual high-five to you for accepting this challenge! Embracing change and the path of self-improvement demands courage, and your commitment to this journey is a testament to yours. Remember, you've totally got this!

Alright, fasten your seatbelt, and let's hit the road! Your thrilling journey of growth begins right here...

Ground rules to win the challenge!

Now before we jump into what you'll be doing day-by-day on the program, let's lay out some rules of the road:

Rule #1: Pace yourself: This is a marathon, not a sprint. So, take your time. The most important part is that you're giving each task your best shot, not how quickly you complete them.

Rule #2: Be honest: Your answers in quizzes and self-assessments are for you, and only you. Be honest. It's all about understanding where you're at so you can figure out where you're going.

Rule #3: Reflect: This isn't a check-the-box situation. After each task, take a few moments to think about what you learned and how you felt. Reflection is key to growth.

Now, let's jump into your 50-day growth mindset program! Remember, you don't have to do it all at once. Spread it out and make it a part of your daily routine.

IT'S A JOURNEY

Day-by-day: your 50-day growth mindset challenge!

Day 1: Know your mindset

Take a "mindset assessment" quiz. This is a simple online questionnaire that will help you understand where you currently stand in terms of fixed and growth mindsets. Try this one at wdhb.com (google "wdhb growth mindset quiz" and it should be one of the first results).

Day 2: Fixed vs growth mindset

What we're going to do today is pretty straightforward. Grab a piece of paper, draw a line down the middle, and make two columns. Label one "fixed mindset" and the other "growth mindset." What we're aiming to do is flesh out examples from your own life where you've shown signs of both mindsets.

For each column, jot down instances where you've shown a fixed or growth mindset. This could be in school, during sports, or even just in your day-to-day life.

Let's say, for instance, you've always thought you're just not a "math person." That goes in the "fixed mindset" column. But remember that time when you were trying to learn how to ride a bike? You didn't get it right away, and you fell over a bunch of times, but you didn't give up. You kept at it, practicing day after day until finally, you were whizzing around like a pro. That's a perfect example for the "growth mindset" column.

This exercise isn't about judging yourself or feeling bad about the times when you've shown a fixed mindset. It's about understanding your thought patterns and realizing where you have room to grow.

The goal is to have more and more entries in that growth mindset column as you become more conscious of your mindset and make the effort to shift from a fixed to a growth mindset. So grab that paper, start reflecting, and remember: this is just another step in your journey toward growth.

Day 3: Growth mindset journaling

So here's the plan. Each night, before you decide to catch some z's for the rest of the challenge, you're going to jot down a few thoughts in this diary. The goal? To delve into your experiences, especially the ones that revolved around challenges, and see what gems you can dig up.

 For today, let's start with something manageable. Write about a time when you stared a challenge in the face and said, "bring it on!" It doesn't have to be something massive. It could be anything that really tested your mettle. And don't forget to include what you took away from the experience.

Let's say you had to give a presentation in class, and public speaking is not really your jam. But you stepped up, added a dash of creativity, and put together a presentation that had people turning their heads. Sure, you stuttered a bit and maybe forgot your lines once or twice, but you did it. You faced your fear.

So how could you put this in your diary? Here's a snippet to get your ideas flowing:

> "Today, I remembered that time I had to present my science project to the whole class. My nerves were off the charts, my palms felt like they'd been dipped in the ocean, and my heart was playing some high-speed techno. But I didn't back down. I practiced, I prepped, and I stepped up to the plate. It was far from flawless. In fact, I fumbled over my words and my notes decided to play 52-card pickup. But when it was over, I felt like a boss. I learned that fear is just a feeling. It doesn't call the shots. Even when I'm shaking in my shoes, I can still rise up. I'm stronger than I sometimes think, and that's a pretty powerful thing to realize."

This diary is going to be your go-to place for all things growth mindset. It's where you'll scribble down your struggles, your wins, your lessons, and all those tiny moments where you notice yourself growing. So grab that pen, flip open your diary, and let's start this amazing journey!

Day 4: The power of yet

You see, 'yet' is like a secret superpower that turns a brick wall into a door. It takes a dead end and pops in a little window. And trust me, it's a game-changer when it comes to nurturing a growth mindset. So, are you ready to see it in action?

First off, grab a piece of paper (or your growth mindset journal) and write down five things that you think you can't do or find really tough. It might be stuff like mastering a particular skateboard trick, acing algebra equations or nailing that super-fast rap part in your favorite song.

Here are a few examples:

1.   I can't play a guitar solo.
2.   I'm not good at public speaking.
3.   I can't beat my high score in that tricky video game.
4.   I can't run a mile without stopping.
5.   I can't cook a decent lasagna.

Alright, now here's where the magic happens. We're going to add the word 'yet' to the end of each statement. Let's see how that transforms our list:

1.   I can't play a guitar solo...yet.
2.   I'm not good at public speaking...yet.
3.   I can't beat my high score in that tricky video game...yet.
4.   I can't run a mile without stopping...yet.
5.   I can't cook a decent lasagna...yet.

Feel that shift? Suddenly, it's not about what you can't do. It's about what you haven't mastered...yet. It opens up a world of possibilities and underlines that you're on a journey of learning and growth. It's not about instant perfection but constant progress.

So, spend a moment reflecting on how this little tweak changes your perspective. Does it make those challenges seem less daunting? Does it spark a little flame of hope? Jot down your thoughts because they're going to be a key part of your growth mindset journey.

Remember, every master was once a beginner, and every pro started as an amateur.

Day 5: Inspirational stories

Today, we're going on an inspirational journey—we're going to delve into the life of a famous personality who's rocked a growth mindset. The best part? We get to see how their life lessons can apply to our own. So, pull up a comfy chair, and let's dive in!

First things first, think about the awesome personalities—perhaps you could start with some of the superstars we chatted about in earlier chapters. But hey, don't limit yourself to just them. The world is brimming with inspiring folks who've embraced a growth mindset. Athletes, artists, scientists, entrepreneurs—the sky's the limit!

Once you've picked your person, do a bit of detective work. Search online, check out books, watch documentaries—gather all the info you can about their journey. What were their struggles? How did they deal with setbacks? What can you learn from their path to success?

Let's say you decide to research Michael Jordan. You might learn that, despite being known as one of the greatest basketball players of all time, Jordan didn't make his high school varsity team on his first try. Yep, you heard right. But did he let that stop him? Not a chance. He practiced like a beast, honed his skills, and kept pushing forward, eventually becoming a legend in his field.

Here's how you might reflect on his story:

1. **What I learned:** even "naturals" have to work hard to succeed. Michael Jordan faced rejection early in his career, but he didn't let that define him. Instead, he used it to fuel his drive to improve.

2. **How I can apply it:** if I don't succeed at something right away, it doesn't mean I'm not good at it or that I can't get better. Like Jordan, I need to embrace practice, patience, and perseverance.

Remember, the best stories are often not about perfect heroes, but about real people who make mistakes, learn, grow, and keep on keeping on. And who knows, one day someone might be researching your story of growth and resilience!

Day 6: Embrace mistakes

 Day 6 is all about owning our mess-ups and using them as stepping stones. We're going to reflect on a recent mistake we've made. But instead of giving ourselves a hard time, we're going to learn from it.

First off, I want you to think about a recent mistake you've made. It doesn't have to be some earth-shattering, end-of-the-world event. It could be something as simple as forgetting to do your homework or accidentally missing a friend's birthday.

Next, you're going to channel your inner Sherlock and really analyze this mistake. Not to beat yourself up about it, but to understand how it happened and how you can avoid it next time.

So, let's imagine you totally forgot to study for a test. You mixed up the dates, and the next thing you knew, you were staring at a bunch of questions you had no idea how to answer. Ouch, right?

Here's how you could reflect on this in your growth mindset journal:

LEARNING FROM MISTAKES = GROWTH

Mistake: mixed up the dates and forgot to study for a test.

What I learned: I need to be more organized with my time and assignments. It's important to double-check the dates for tests and assignments.

How I can do better next time: I can start using a planner or digital calendar to keep track of important dates. Also, a regular study schedule could help me be more prepared, so I'm not cramming at the last minute.

See what we did there? Instead of focusing on the negative (the messed-up test), we're shifting our attention to what we can learn and how we can improve. So, take a leap, embrace your mistakes, and discover how you can turn them into your secret weapons for success.

Remember, every mistake is an opportunity to learn something new. So grab that chance and let your growth mindset shine through!

Day 7: Seek out challenges

On Day 7, we're going to step out of our comfort zone and face a new challenge head-on. Remember, there's no growth in the comfort zone and no comfort in the growth zone. So, it's time to get a little uncomfortable and seek out a challenge that pushes our boundaries. Are you game?

Let's break it down:

Step 1: Decide on your challenge

This is entirely up to you, but here's the key: pick something that feels a bit out of your league. Maybe there's a challenging recipe you've been avoiding because it seems too intricate, or perhaps there's a tricky puzzle that's been gathering dust on your shelf. Or hey, maybe it's time to strike up a conversation with that new kid in school who seems pretty cool, but you've just been too shy to approach. Whatever it is, it should feel a little challenging—just enough to make your heart race a little.

Step 2: Dive into the challenge

Alright, now that you've picked your challenge, it's time to jump right in! Remember, the goal isn't to nail it perfectly—it's to try something new and learn from the experience. So, if you're cooking that complex dish and your first attempt doesn't exactly look like the picture in the cookbook, that's alright. If the puzzle has you stumped after a few attempts, no biggie. The important thing is that you're pushing yourself and trying something different.

Step 3: Reflect on your experience

Once you've tackled the challenge, it's time for a little reflection. Grab your growth mindset journal and jot down some thoughts. How did the challenge make you feel? What did you learn from it? Even if you didn't succeed as you hoped, what did the attempt teach you?

Here's an example:

Challenge: strike up a conversation with the new student in my class.

Experience: at first, I felt pretty nervous and wasn't sure what to say. But once we started talking, it got easier. We ended up having a great conversation about our favorite books.

What I learned: trying something new can be nerve-wracking, but it can also be rewarding. I learned that I can overcome my shyness and make new friends.

 Remember, seeking out challenges is a surefire way to grow. So push your boundaries, step out of your comfort zone, and watch how you bloom.

Day 8: The growth mindset pledge

Welcome, welcome to Day 8, my friend! Now, it's time to go ahead and make things, like, official. We're going to put pen to paper and declare our commitment to this awesome thing we've been exploring—the growth mindset.

Here's how we're going to do this:

Step 1: The rearview mirror

Alright, before we get going, grab that growth mindset journal of yours. Flip through the past entries. It's like a time travel journey, seeing where you started and where you are now. Soak in the insights, the growth, and even the small shifts in how you see things.

Step 2: Your promise to you

Next, it's time to write your pledge. Think of it as a promise you're making to yourself—a vow that you'll stick with the whole growth, resilience, and never-give-up attitude. It's your pledge, so make sure it rings true to you.

For example, it could go like this: "I vow to face the tough stuff head-on, to look for lessons in my blunders, and to never stop reaching for better, no matter what comes my way."

Step 3: Make it official

Now, it's time to make it real. Write down your growth mindset pledge in your journal. Make it stand out—underline it, doodle around it, make it bold—whatever works for you!

Step 4: Take it in

After you've put it all down on paper, just sit with it for a bit. Reflect on what you've written. Does it get your pulse racing? Make you feel pumped and a little bit like you've accepted a dare? Perfect! That's what commitment to growth feels like.

For instance:

My pledge: "I commit to embracing challenges, learning lessons from my failures, and always pushing the envelope. I'm all about growth, and resilience is my secret sauce."

Reflection: Scribbling down this pledge, it's kind of electrifying. It's a reminder that it's perfectly cool to goof up and face challenges as long as I'm learning, improving, and reaching for more.

Your very own growth mindset pledge is a personal commitment, a kind of north star that's there to remind you of the journey you're on. Keep it close and let it be your driving force.

Day 9: Develop a new skill

Today's challenge is seriously going to shake things up. We're about to embark on an exciting mission of acquiring a new skill. Sounds intriguing, right? It's all about expanding our horizons and putting our growth mindset into action. So, if you're game (and I bet you are), let's jump into it!

Step 1: Choose your skill

Alright, it's time to think about that skill you've always dreamed of mastering. Could be anything under the sun! Maybe it's cooking or coding? Perhaps you've always wanted to grow your own tomatoes or master a gnarly skateboard trick? The sky's the limit here! For our example, let's say we're keen on learning how to strum a guitar.

Step 2: Understand the basics

 Now, let's get our hands dirty with a bit of research. Get the lowdown on the basics of your chosen skill. For instance, if it's the guitar, you might want to familiarize yourself with the anatomy of a guitar, how to read guitar tabs, and a few beginner's chords.

Step 3: Formulate a smart goal

Now, this is where we set our sights on turning our "I wish" into an "I can." Remember the drill about smart goals? They're specific, measurable, achievable, relevant, and time-bound. Use the template to make it visual! This will help you set a clear and precise goal for your new skill.

So, if we're sticking with the guitar, a smart goal could look like this: "I'll learn to play 'Happy Birthday' on the guitar within the next 15 days."

Step 4: Break it up

Okay, now comes the cool part—breaking that goal into manageable chunks. Believe me, things seem less daunting when you tackle them step-by-step. Plus, the sweet feeling of accomplishment with each completed step will keep you pumped!

If we're talking guitar, your breakdown could look something like this:

1. Research and understand the parts of a guitar and the correct way to hold it—Day 1.

2. Get a grasp on reading guitar tabs—Day 2.

3. Start practicing the tabs for 'Happy Birthday'—Days 3-7.

4. Keep practicing until I can play the tune smoothly—Days 8-15.

And voila! You're on the right track to mastering a new skill while growing your mindset. Remember, it's all about the journey and the growth along the way. Embrace the challenges, learn from the bloopers, and above all, enjoy the process!

Day 10: Reflection day

Reflect on the last ten days. What activities did you enjoy? What did you learn about yourself? Write a journal entry about your thoughts and feelings.

REFLECT, LEARN, GROW: A REFLECTION GUIDE

WHAT WENT WELL?

WHAT WAS CHALLENGING?

HOW WILL I IMPROVE?

Day 11: Visualizing success

Welcome to Day 11 of our mind-growing journey. Today, we're gonna dive
deep into the power of visualization. We're gonna channel some serious mental
energy to picture ourselves conquering that awesome skill we chose back on
Day 9.

Step 1: Find your Zen space

First things first, find a quiet, comfortable spot where you won't be disturbed.
This is gonna be your personal visualization haven. It could be your bedroom,
the garden, or even a cozy corner of the living room. The goal here is to have a
chill zone where your imagination can run wild.

Step 2: Close your eyes and focus

Now that you've found your Zen space, it's time to close your eyes
and take a few deep breaths. Feel the air filling your lungs, and
then slowly release it. This will help calm your mind and focus your
thoughts. You're about to go on a mental adventure!

Step 3: Start the journey

Picture yourself diving into your new skill. Using our guitar example from Day
9, visualize holding the guitar, your fingers on the strings. Imagine the sound
it makes as you strum for the first time. Really try to feel it, the vibrations, the
melody—it's as if you're really there.

Step 4: Tackling the challenges

Now comes the interesting part. Visualize the obstacles you
might face. Maybe it's a tricky chord that just seems impossible to get right.
But hey, remember, you've got that growth mindset! Visualize yourself practicing that chord, again and again, getting
a bit better each time.

Step 5: Celebrating the victory

And now, the best part. Imagine yourself finally mastering that tricky chord,
playing the whole 'Happy Birthday' tune smoothly. Can you feel a sense of
accomplishment? That's you! You've done it in your mind, and with time and
effort, you'll do it in reality, too!

Spend around 15 minutes on this visualization exercise. Really try to get into
it, immerse yourself in the experience. It's your journey, your adventure.

Remember, seeing is believing, and by visualizing your success, you're already halfway there!

Remember to jot down your experience in your growth mindset journal! Trust me, you'll love to look back at these notes one day.

Day 12: Replace negative self-talk

Welcome to Day 12, where we're gonna confront something we all do a bit more often than we'd like to admit: negative self-talk. Yep, those moments when we're our own worst critics. Today, we're turning those not-so-nice chats into our own personal pep talks. So, are you ready to take control of that inner voice? Alright, let's get to it!

Step 1: Detective mode on
Today, your task is to play detective and catch your inner critic red-handed. Pay attention to your thoughts throughout the day. Do you find yourself thinking things like "I'm no good at this," or "I always mess up"? Write them down, every single one. No judgment here, just observing.

Step 2: Make the swap
Alright, so now you've got your list of Debbie Downer declarations. It's time for a remodel! For each negative statement, craft a positive, growth-focused counterpart. For example, "I'm no good at this" can be transformed into "I'm learning and improving at this every day."

Step 3: Repeat and replace
Now that you've turned your negatives into positives, your job is to start using them. Every time you catch yourself slipping into negative self-talk, stop and swap it out for its positive replacement. It might feel weird at first, but stick with it. Before long, it'll start to come naturally.

To illustrate this with an example, let's say you're working on a challenging math problem and find yourself thinking, "I'm just not a math person." Stop right there! Swap it out for "math can be tough for me, but that just means I have to approach it differently and keep trying. I'm capable of learning and mastering this."

Today's task is a powerful one. **By changing the narrative in our heads, we're training ourselves to think and react with a growth mindset, even when** things get tough. Remember, your inner voice should be your biggest cheer-leader, not your harshest critic.

Keep jotting down your experiences in your growth mindset journal. This journey of self-discovery and growth you're on is something to be proud of, and every step is worth remembering.

Day 13: Peer inspiration

You've been on a roll so far, and I'm stoked to see you still here, ready to keep growing. Today, we're gonna switch things up a bit by seeking some outside inspiration. You're not alone on this growth journey, and there are heaps of people in your life who can offer wisdom, encouragement, and a fresh perspective. Let's dive into it!

Step 1: Scouting the growth mindset

First up, it's time to think about the people in your life. Who comes to mind when you think about someone who's not afraid of challenges, who learns from mistakes, and who's always eager to grow? Could be a buddy, a sibling, a teacher, or even your skateboarding coach. Got someone in mind? Great!

Step 2: Heart-to-heart session

Next, reach out to this person. If you can, catch up over a snack or a walk in the park. Tell them about this awesome growth mindset journey you're on and ask if they've got time for a little chat. This isn't an interview—more like two pals sharing thoughts and experiences.

Step 3: Key takeaways

During your chat, listen closely to their experiences and how they approach challenges. Ask them about a time they really struggled with something and how they worked through it. Don't forget to jot down what you learn—these nuggets of wisdom are pure gold!

For example, let's say you chose your older cousin Mia, who's always aced her piano recitals. You've admired her performances, but today, you learn about the hours of practice, the missed notes, the moments of doubt, and how she pushed through it all. She shares how she uses her mistakes as stepping stones, not stumbling blocks, and how she views each practice session as an opportunity to improve. Powerful stuff, right?

Scribble these insights into your growth mindset journal. Reflect on how you can apply what you learned from Mia (or whoever your growth mindset maestro is) to your own life and journey.

Remember, everyone's growth journey is unique, but we can gain so much by sharing and learning from each other. So, here's to Day 13, a day filled with learning, sharing, and growing together!

Day 14: Get set, fitness challenge!

Today is all about stretching those muscles and breaking a little sweat. We're diving into a fitness challenge. But hang on, we aren't expecting you to transform into a top-tier athlete overnight. It's about setting a reasonable fitness goal and working towards it step by step.

Consider this, is there a physical activity you've always wanted to do better? Perhaps running that extra mile, perfecting a yoga pose, or even scoring a perfect goal? Great! That's your challenge. The focus here isn't about hitting a home run right away, it's all about seeing how you grow stronger and better over time, just like your mindset.

Sure, the exercise will give you a nice dose of 'feel good' endorphins. But what's even cooler is how this activity gives you a front-row seat to see the growth mindset in action. Your body, much like your brain, gets better with practice. You start, you stumble, you progress, and before you know it, you've nailed it!

So, tie up those laces, roll out your mat, or grab that ball, and let's get started. No stress, remember? It's all about baby steps. Set your goal, give it your best, and take note of your progress. You've got this! Let's make fitness a fun part of our growth journey.

Day 15: Master of adaptability

Let's dive into the wild and wacky world of adaptability today. Now, don't be fooled by the big word, it's all about rolling with the punches, bouncing back from curveballs, and basically handling whatever life decides to toss your way.

Step 1: Flashback to a challenge you faced

Let's start by time-traveling back to a recent unexpected situation or challenge you faced. Maybe it was that surprise test in history, or the time your bestie couldn't make it to your big game, or perhaps the internet went out just when you had a massive assignment due. Remember how that felt? Unsettling, right? But you're here, you made it!

Step 2: Chart your adaptability journey

Next, pull out your growth mindset journal. It's time to spill the beans about that incident. Write down how you adapted to that unexpected situation. How did you handle it?

Let's say your challenge was the surprise history test. Initially, you might have panicked a bit, but then you remembered your study sessions and class notes. You adapted by calming your nerves, remembering what you had learned, and doing your best on the test.

Step 3: Reflection time

Finally, think about what you learned from the whole experience. Did you realize that you're more prepared than you give yourself credit for? Or maybe you found out that it's crucial to have a backup plan, like saving your work in two places when you're relying on the internet.

In the case of the surprise history test, you might have learned that regular study sessions really paid off, or maybe you realized that panicking at first is okay as long as you can calm down and refocus quickly.

Remember, life loves to throw unexpected plot twists our way. But being adaptable means you can handle them and even use them as opportunities for growth. So, here's to bending, not breaking, and becoming masters of adaptability!

Day 16: The feedback loop

Yeah, I know asking for and getting feedback can be a bit awkward, but hear me out. Feedback, especially the constructive kind, is like a secret shortcut to becoming better. And remember, it's never a personal attack. It's about helping you level up.

For today's challenge, we're diving headfirst into the world of constructive criticism. Here's what you gotta do:

1. First off, think about something you've been working on lately. It could be your basketball shooting technique, your painting skills, your baking recipes, or even your coding abilities.

2. Next, find someone who knows a thing or two about your chosen skill. It could be a teacher, a coach, a parent, a sibling, or even a good friend.

3. Now, this is where you gotta be brave. Approach them and ask if they wouldn't mind giving you some feedback on that specific skill you're working on. **Be sure to make it clear you're looking for ways to improve, not just a pat on the back.** So, instead of asking something like "what do you think of my dribbling?" Go for a more precise question like "do you have any tips on how I can improve my dribbling technique?"

4. This next step might be the hardest one: just listen. Try to keep an open mind and don't rush to defend yourself. They're trying to help you, remember? Oh, and don't forget to say thanks!

5. Once the feedback session is done, grab your trusty journal. Write down what they told you, and right next to it, write down how you can put that feedback into action.

For example, if you asked your coach about your basketball shooting technique and they suggested working on your shooting form, you could write something like:

Feedback: work on shooting form.

Action plan: practice shooting drills focusing on form.

And there you have it! You've just navigated your way through the feedback loop—seeking feedback, receiving it, and making an action plan to improve.

Day 17: Count your growth blessings

You know how everyone is always talking about gratitude and how it's all the rage? Well, it's popular for a reason. So, let's take a break from our daily grind and take a moment to recognize and appreciate the growth journey you're on.

Here's your mission for the day:

1. Grab your trusty growth mindset journal. Don't have it on hand? No problem! A scrap of paper will work just fine.

2. At the top of the page, jot down: "Growth Blessings."

3. Now, write out things that you're genuinely thankful for on this growth mindset journey. These could be people who've inspired you, interesting books you've discovered, or the tricky obstacles that have toughened you up.

You might jot down something like this:

"Grateful for my math teacher who makes challenges feel like growth opportunities."

"Feeling thankful for my friend Zoe, who's always down for a chat about the cool growth mindset stuff we're learning."

"Grateful for that head-scratching coding problem that showed me I'm more tenacious and resourceful than I gave myself credit for."

4. Try to count at least five blessings. Really think about each one and feel the gratitude.

5. Once you've finished, take a step back and take a look at your list. That right there is your personal cheer squad and fuel for your growth mindset journey.

And hey, this gratitude thing isn't a one-time deal. Whenever you're feeling stuck or a bit down, take a moment to remind yourself of all the awesome things on your gratitude list. It might just give you the mood boost and perspective shift you need.

Day 18: Take on a leadership role

Being a leader isn't just about bossing people around. No, being a leader is about stepping up, taking responsibility, making tough calls, and being there for your team. Sounds intense? It is! But it's also a fantastic way to stretch your growth mindset muscles.

Here's the plan:

1. **Find an opportunity to be a leader today.** It doesn't have to be big, like becoming the president of your school. Look for something a little smaller scale, yet meaningful.

Maybe you can lead a study group for that tricky history test coming up. Or you could step up as the captain in a game of basketball at the local park. Or maybe your drama club needs a director for their next play. These all count!

2. **Now that you're in the driver's seat, take a moment to reflect on how it feels.** It might be a bit scary, a little thrilling, and definitely challenging. Write down these feelings in your journal.

For example, "being the study group leader was a bit nerve-wracking. I was worried about getting the facts right and managing the group. But I also felt a sense of accomplishment when I was able to explain complex concepts to my friends."

3. Next, focus on how this leadership experience is pushing you to grow. Are you becoming better at organizing? Improving your communication skills? Learning to handle disagreements more effectively? Jot down these observations in your journal.

You might write something like, "I realized that being a leader means more than just being in charge. It's about listening, coordinating, and motivating others. I'm definitely getting better at communicating my ideas clearly."

Remember, even if you face setbacks or challenges, don't sweat it. They're all part of the learning experience.

Day 19: Reflection day

Reflect on your growth mindset journey so far. Write a journal entry about your thoughts, feelings, and learnings. Do you feel a change in your mindset? What are the areas you think you've grown in?

Day 20: Growth vs fixed mindset in media

Ever notice how much TV, movies, and books influence our thoughts and beliefs? It's true—media has a massive impact on how we perceive the world, including how we view the concepts of growth and fixed mindsets.

Today, your mission is to become a mindset detective. Here's your three-step plan to get that ball rolling:

1. **Choose your media:** It could be that new Netflix series you've been binge-watching, the novel you're reading for English class, or even a news article online.

2. **Watch or read attentively:** Pay special attention to how the characters or people handle setbacks, make progress, or face challenges. Are they demonstrating a growth mindset (think: perseverance, learning from failure, and believing in the power to improve)? Or are they showing signs of a fixed mindset (like giving up when things get tough or believing that their abilities are set in stone)?

For instance, let's take Harry Potter from... well, Harry Potter. When he's learning to cast spells, he messes up a bunch, but does he give up? Nope! He keeps practicing, learning, and growing. That's a growth mindset in action.

3. **Share and discuss:** Next, grab a friend, sibling, or parent and share your findings. Discuss how the media portrays these mindsets and how it impacts the story or message.

You could say, "I noticed that Harry showed a real growth mindset when he was learning magic. Even though he wasn't a natural at it, he put in the effort and kept improving. It made me realize that even if something is difficult at first, I can get better with practice."

By doing this activity, you'll become more aware of how growth and fixed mindsets are represented all around us. Plus, you're sharpening your skills at spotting these mindsets in action.

Day 21: Setting small goals

Okay, think back to Day 9. Remember that super cool skill you picked? Let's chat about that. How's it going? Are you sticking to the plan or has it been a little trickier than expected? Either way, it's totally fine. We're all about growing here, and sometimes, growth means tweaking the game plan a bit.

Today, your mission is all about making your big goal feel less overwhelming by breaking it down into smaller, super-achievable mini-goals. Let's do this!

1. **Reality check:** First, do a quick status update. Are you making progress with your big goal? Maybe you're learning to code, and you've managed to understand some basic syntax. Or perhaps things have been a bit slow, and you need to spend more time practicing. That's okay too! No judgments here, just jot down what's up.

2. **Set mini-goals:** Now, it's time to get specific. Set three mini-goals related to your skill. Make sure they're super clear (you know exactly what you need to do), measurable (you can definitely tell when you've done it), and time-bound (you've got a deadline).

For instance, if you're learning how to play the guitar, a mini-goal could be: "practice the G chord for 10 minutes each day for the next seven days." It's clear what you need to do (practice the G chord), you can measure your progress (did you practice for 10 minutes?), And it's time-bound (you have a week to do it).

3. **Write 'em down:** Write these mini-goals down in your journal. Seeing them on paper makes them real and gives you a clear path forward.

Remember, small steps lead to big wins. These mini-goals are like checkpoints on your way to mastering your skill. So don't worry if your big goal feels a little daunting right now. Just focus on these smaller goals, and you'll be making progress before you know it.

Day 22: Flip the script

We're going to talk about a word that a lot of us might not like: failure. Yeah, it's got a bad rap, but here's the kicker—it's actually a stealthy little teacher in disguise. Yep, you heard that right. Failure, as much as it might sting at the time, is actually packed with lessons.

So, today, we're going on a bit of a time trip. Take a moment to think of a time when you fell flat on your face. Maybe it was that math test that you bombed or the soccer game where you missed the goal. Got that memory? Alright, hold onto it.

Now, grab your trusty journal and a pen. We're going to write a two-paragraph epic about this experience. Don't worry, this isn't English class, no grades here, just real talk.

1. **The Epic Fail:** In the first paragraph, we're setting the scene. Give a quick rundown of what happened. Remember, it's not about beating yourself up over it, but about understanding what went wrong. So, keep it factual and straight-up. Something like, "I had a math test on fractions. I thought I was ready, but when I got the paper, my mind blanked out. I couldn't solve most of the problems, and I ended up failing the test."

2. **The Fantastic Flip:** Now, this is where the magic happens. In the second paragraph, we're going to flip the script. Write about what this epic fail taught you. Did it show you a weak spot you need to work on? Or maybe it taught you about preparation or time management? This could look something like, "failing the math test showed me that I struggle with fractions. But more than that, it taught me that I need to change how I prepare

for tests. I can't just read through my notes, I need to practice problems too. That way, I'm more prepared for whatever the test throws at me."

By doing this, you're changing how you see failure. It's not just about losing or not being good enough. It's about learning, growing, and becoming better. So let's turn those epic fails into fantastic flips, alright?

Day 23: Positivity Jar

Today we're doing something super fun: we're making a Positivity Jar. Sounds cool, right? And trust me, it's as exciting as it sounds.

First things first: you'll need a jar. Any jar. It could be an old coffee canister, an empty jam jar, whatever you've got lying around. Got your jar? Awesome. Now, here's what you're going to do with it.

Every time something good happens, something that made you feel like a rockstar, even if it's teeny-tiny, you're going to write it down on a piece of paper. It doesn't have to be an essay—a simple sentence will do. Maybe you finally nailed that complicated equation in your math homework. Or perhaps you managed to jog non-stop for 5 more minutes than usual. Whatever it is, write it down, fold that paper up, and pop it into the jar. This jar is about to become your visual high-five, a celebration of your victories, big and small.

Let's play this out: Suppose you're learning to play the guitar. And after a week of trying, you finally play the intro to your favorite song without messing up. That's a win! So, grab a pen and jot down: "played the intro to [your favorite song] perfectly on the guitar!" Fold that paper and pop it in the jar.

Watching your positivity jar fill up with wins is like watching your growth mindset in action. It's a constant reminder that you're evolving, changing, and most importantly, growing.

Give it a try, and let the wins pile up!

Day 24: Peer teaching

How cool is it when you learn something new and then get to show it off? Well, today we're doing just that, but with a twist—we're becoming teachers!

Think of something cool you've recently learned. Maybe it's that nifty Photoshop trick, or the steps to solve a quadratic equation, or how to bake the best chocolate chip cookies (because who doesn't love cookies?). Whatever it is, your mission for today is to pass that knowledge on to someone else. You could choose a friend, your little sibling, or even one of your parents.

Teaching someone else is not just about sharing knowledge; it's also an excellent way to reinforce what you've learned. It can help you understand the concept or skill better and remember it longer. Plus, it's a pretty cool way to boost your confidence and communication skills.

Let's say you've been learning to play a new song on your guitar. You've finally got the hang of it and can play it smoothly. Awesome! Now, grab your sibling or a friend who's interested in guitar and show them how to play it. Walk them through the chords, the strumming pattern, the whole nine yards. When they get stuck, help them out. And when they finally play it right, celebrate that moment!

Once you're done with your impromptu guitar lesson, take some time to reflect. How did it feel to teach someone? Did it help you understand the song better? Write down your thoughts in your growth mindset journal.

Remember, being able to teach something shows you've really got it down. So kudos to you, professor you! You're growing, one lesson at a time.

Day 25: Mindful moments

Practice mindfulness for 15 minutes. This could be through meditation, a mindful walk, simply focusing on your breath, or the mindfulness exercises we laid out in chapter 9. Reflect on how this helps you stay focused and open to growth.

Day 26: "Talk the walk" role-playing

Let's get a little theatrical today! You know, it's one thing to read and understand a growth mindset, and it's a whole other ball game to actually "live it."

Today, you are going to bring your understanding of a growth mindset to life with a fun role-playing exercise!

You're going to create a short skit or a scenario where you're faced with a challenging situation. This could be anything from getting a low grade on a test, losing a game, struggling with learning a new skill, or any other challenge you have experienced or can think of.

Now, here's the catch: you're going to act out this scenario twice. The first time, you'll react with a fixed mindset. Feel free to exaggerate your reactions, get dramatic, and really embody that "I can't do this" attitude.

 But then, we rewind. You'll act out the same scenario again, but this time, you'll respond with a growth mindset. Show how you can accept the challenge, how you learn from failure, and how you keep pushing forward despite obstacles.

You can perform this skit alone, or involve your friends or family. You can even video record it if you like. It's a great way to visualize and internalize how a growth mindset can change the way we handle challenges.

Remember, this activity isn't about being a top-notch actor. It's about understanding and embodying the growth mindset. Plus, it's a great way to have some fun while doing so!

Once you're done, reflect on the differences between the two mindsets. How did you feel when acting out each mindset? Which mindset do you want to embrace in your life?

So, ready to get dramatic? Lights, camera, action, and grow!

Day 27: Exploring new perspectives

Ever heard that old saying "walk a mile in someone else's shoes?" Today's your chance to do just that but with words. Your mission for today, if you choose to accept it, is to have a chinwag with someone who has a different perspective from yours. Could be about anything, really. A controversial book, a hot topic, or just the latest viral video.

 Here's the catch, though. You're not there to debate or convince them. You're there to listen and learn. Yes, even if you totally disagree with them. Because remember, the growth mindset isn't just about skills and challenges, it's also about understanding and empathy.

So, find someone who fits the bill. Maybe your history buff grandpa who always disagrees with your take on World War II, or your best friend who thinks that pineapple on pizza is an absolute abomination (or a delight, depending on where you stand on that debate).

Once you've had your chat, jot down what you learned. What new insights did you get from seeing things from their angle? How did it challenge your own views? Did it maybe, just maybe, change your mind a bit?

For instance, let's say you had a conversation with your cousin about climate change. You've always been a bit skeptical about it, but your cousin's a hardcore climate activist. After talking to her and hearing about the research she's done, the people she's met, and the changes she's seen, you might start to see things differently. You might even feel motivated to take action in your own way.

No matter how big or small, any change in your perspective means you're growing.

Day 28: Reflection day

 Reflect on the last 4 weeks. Write a journal entry about your thoughts, feelings, and learning. Celebrate the progress you've made and set goals for the next phase of your journey!

Day 29: Experiment extravaganza!

So, who's up for playing a bit of detective today? We've all seen those amazing science experiments online or in class that leave us thinking, "woah, how did they do that?" Well, guess what? Today's your chance to don your lab coat (metaphorically, of course) and dive into your very own experiment!

Here's the fun part: you get to pick what you want to experiment with. It could be a simple science experiment, like testing which type of soil plants grow best in, or even a social experiment, like observing how people react to acts of kindness. The goal isn't to cause a massive chemical explosion or change the world (yet), but to develop your critical thinking and problem-solving skills.

Once you've picked your experiment, it's time to get into action. What's your hypothesis, or the outcome you think might happen? Jot that down. Now go ahead and conduct your experiment, making sure to note your observations along the way. Once it's done, compare the results with your hypothesis. Did things turn out as you expected, or were you surprised? Either way, you've just made progress on your growth mindset journey, using your curiosity, creativity, and problem-solving skills!

Today's activity is a perfect reminder that growth is all about trying new things, taking risks, and learning from the results. Whether your hypothesis was right or wrong, you've learned something new, and that's a win in our book! So, get out there, and let's start experimenting!

Day 30: Public speaking challenge

Have you ever had so much to say about something you're totally into, but just kept it to yourself? Well, today is the day to let it out! It's all about impromptu speaking. Yup, you heard it right. We're going off the cuff and straight from the heart.

Choose something you are passionate about. It could be the new band you can't stop listening to, that book series you're engrossed in, or even your thoughts on climate change. Your subject can be whatever gets your heart racing and your words flowing.

Next, gather your family or friends. Or both. Let them know you're taking the floor for the next five minutes. Yes, you read it right—five minutes. Might seem a little scary now, but hey, remember Day 1? We're all about facing those fears!

Don't worry about preparing a script. This isn't about being perfectly polished. It's about speaking from the heart, sharing what you love, and communicating it effectively.

Once you're done, reflect on how it went. How did it feel to share your passion out loud? Did you stumble over words, or did it flow easily? Did you keep your audience engaged? Did you speak clearly and confidently?

Let's say you chose to talk about your favorite video game, and in your excitement, you stumbled a bit on your words, but your friends were hooked on to every word you said because of the passion in your voice. That's a win right there!

Remember, public speaking is a valuable skill, one that's going to serve you well in all walks of life.

Day 31: Exploring careers

Alright, let's take a break from the present and hop into a time machine. Destination? Your future. Specifically, let's focus on what kind of career you might want to dive into.

We all have interests, right? Things that make us feel alive and spark our curiosity. Maybe you love music and can see yourself as a music producer, or you're really into animals and could totally rock being a vet. Or perhaps, you're a math wiz and a career in data science seems like the perfect fit.

So, here's what you gotta do. Pick three careers that pique your interest. They could be anything, from a professional esports player to an astronaut. Then, do a little bit of detective work. Dig into what these jobs are really like, what skills and qualities they demand.

For example, if you want to be a writer, you'd need strong creativity, a good grasp of language, the ability to express ideas clearly, and a lot of patience (because let's be honest, writer's block is a real pain).

Next, take a look at yourself. Do you have these skills and qualities? If yes, awesome! You're on the right track. If not, no worries. Remember, skills can be learned and qualities can be developed. Plan out how you can acquire or strengthen these traits.

And hey, if you're thinking "I have no idea where to start," don't stress it. We've got you covered. Check out our book, *The Essential Career Planning Handbook for Teens*. It's jam-packed with practical advice to help you explore your career options and make decisions that align with your interests, talents, and dreams. So, get researching and start envisioning where your future might take you!

Day 32: Whipping up a growth mindset

Ready for a fun twist to the growth mindset challenge? Today, we're swapping books and quizzes for pots and pans. Why? Because cooking, believe it or not, is a lot like cultivating a growth mindset.

Imagine cooking like a video game. Each level you cross, each recipe you nail, is a win. But the real game-changer is when the dish doesn't turn out quite as expected. Like when the pasta is too al dente or the cake is a bit too dense. Instead of throwing in the towel, that's when you level up in the game of growth mindset.

So here's your challenge: pick a recipe you've never tried before. It could be anything, from pasta to pastries. Don't worry if it looks a bit tricky. Remember, the fun is in figuring it out!

Let's say you decide to bake a cake for the first time. You follow the recipe, but it comes out denser than you wanted. Bummer, right? But hold on, don't quit just yet! This is where your growth mindset kicks in. Instead of deciding "baking's not my thing," think about what might have gone wrong. Did you overmix the batter, making the cake lose its fluffiness? Bingo! You just learned a super important baking lesson for next time.

While you're cooking, reflect on your journey. What does it feel like to dive into something new? What roadblocks did you hit, and how did you push past them? What would you change for the next try?

Here's the thing—cooking, just like the growth mindset, is all about effort, practice, and a sprinkle of patience. Each time you cook, you learn something new, you get better. So, strap on that apron and get cooking! Your growth mindset journey is about to get delicious!

Day 33: Positive affirmations

Alright, are you ready for a small experiment? It's about positive affirmations. Yep, you might have heard of them. They're like these powerful, personal cheerleading chants. They might sound a bit, well, unusual at first. But stick with us here.

Affirmations are not just feel-good quotes you find on social media. These are your own crafted power statements, rooted in the now. They're positive,  they're personal, and they're present tense. They could be something like, "I am braver than I think," or "I have what it takes to conquer my challenges."

So here's what you gotta do: write down three affirmations that really vibe with you. Once you've got them down, your challenge for the next week is to repeat them to yourself every morning when you wake up. Yes, it might feel kind of strange at first, and that's alright. Remember, this whole journey is about exploring new territories, right?

Now, for the next part. After you've had your morning meet-up with your affirmations, spend a moment to note down how you're feeling in your journal.

Maybe you're pumped. Maybe you're feeling a little odd. Maybe you don't feel much different. And guess what? All of that is totally cool. Just jot it down.

As the days go by, you might start noticing some shifts in your mindset, all thanks to these positive self-cheers. So, craft your affirmations, and kickstart your day with a little self-pep talk! You're in for a positive surprise.

Day 34: The power of persistence

Okay, ready for a real test of your willpower? Today's challenge is all about pushing your limits and embracing the art of never giving up. The Japanese have a term for this—it's called "Ganbaru," and it's the spirit of persistence and resilience.

Now, think of something you've been finding pretty tough—a math problem that's been bugging you, a piece of code that keeps hitting errors, a tricky riff on the guitar that you can't seem to get right, or even a level in a video game that you've been stuck on. Yeah, it's been annoying, right? But today's the day you're gonna say "not today!"

Get yourself geared up and dive straight into it. **Don't stop until you've cracked it.** Sounds intimidating? Of course, it's not gonna be a walk in the park. You might wanna scream or even feel like throwing in the towel. But remind yourself—this is your moment of growth.

Let's imagine you've been struggling with a particular basketball move. Today, you could decide, "I'm not leaving this court until I've nailed this move!" Get the ball, take your position, and start. Missed the first shot? No problem. Keep going. The fifth shot went haywire? It's all good. Keep practicing. Every miss is one step closer to the hit.

Once you've conquered the beast (and you will!), Sit back and take a moment to revel in your victory. Reflect on your journey—the ups, the downs, the frustrations, and finally, the sweet taste of success. What kept you going when you wanted to quit? How did this experience of persisting change your understanding of your capabilities?

Write it all down. This record of your triumph over a tough task is a powerful reminder for future challenges. It's proof that you've got what it takes to hang in there, even when the going gets tough. So, put on your persistence cape, it's time to conquer!

Day 35: Reflection day

 Reflect on your journey over the past 35 days. Write a journal entry about your experiences, what you learned, and how you're feeling. Remember, every step forward, no matter how small, is progress!

Keep going, you're doing great! The more you practice, the stronger your growth mindset will become.

Day 36: Deep dive into a topic

Today is all about finding new territories, stretching your mind, and sparking some serious curiosity. Here's the challenge: you're gonna pick a topic that you know absolutely nada about and get on a full-day adventure to learn about it.

Let's say, for instance, you chose something wildly different like 'space travel.' Okay, so where do you start? You can hit up some interesting articles on the internet, watch a couple of documentaries or space vlogs, or listen to podcasts from astronauts or scientists. Maybe even catch up with that crazy 'Mars Rover Twitter account (if it's still rolling around). The sky's not the limit anymore!

You're gonna start at zero, zip, zilch. But that's part of the thrill, isn't it? You might feel a bit lost at first, but slowly, as you begin to connect the dots, you'll see the fog lifting. Note down this roller coaster of a journey in your journal. Was it confusing at first? Did it gradually become interesting? Was it like solving a mystery? Or did it feel like navigating a maze?

The focus here is not just on what you're learning, but also on how you're learning. Feeling a bit disoriented, challenged, and even a tad frustrated is part of the game when you're trying to crack open something new. But remember, it's all part of the bigger journey toward growth and learning. So, get set, strap in, and launch into the cosmos of a new topic!

Day 37: Embrace uncertainty

Today, it's time again to try something that makes you feel butter-flies in your stomach!

Let's give you an example to make this easier. Imagine public speaking is your kryptonite. Even the thought of it makes your hands clammy, right? Well, today, you'll face that fear. You could organize a mini-presentation for your family or friends. You might talk about that topic you recently deep-dived into

or share your opinion on a trendy social issue. It'll be just you, maybe a make-shift mic (a hairbrush works great), and your mini-audience.

Now, it could be nerve-wracking, with shaky hands and a jittery voice, but that's all part of the process. Remember, even the greatest orators had a day one. So, once you're done with this heart-pounding experience, take some time to reflect on it.

How did it feel to confront your fear? Did your heart rate feel like it was sprinting? Were you a bundle of nerves or did you feel an unexpected rush? And, crucially, what did you learn from this experience? Maybe you discovered it wasn't as hair-raising as you anticipated, or you found areas to work on for next time.

The idea here is that when you dare to step into the unknown, you're creating space for personal growth. So, inhale courage, face the uncertainty, and allow it to mold you into a more resilient, courageous version of yourself!

Day 38: Unleash your inner explorer!

Today, we're taking our growth mindset journey outdoors. Yup, you read that right! We're swapping textbooks for trees, classrooms for clouds, and the humdrum routine for a hint of the wild. Ready for an exciting adventure? Let's go!

Here's what you need to do: pick a spot in nature that you've always wanted to explore. It could be a trail at your local park, a nearby beach, or even a scenic neighborhood walk. Wherever it is, it's your expedition for the day.

Now, remember, this is not just about taking a leisurely stroll (although, that's totally cool too!). It's about soaking in the beauty around you, observing, learning, and adapting, just like nature does. Check out the different types of plants or spot some wildlife. Observe the patterns in the clouds or listen to the orchestra of sounds.

Try to understand how everything in nature adapts and evolves to survive and flourish—that's a classic case of a growth mindset in action! See a tree with half its branches chopped off but still blooming? That's resilience! Notice different animals working in teams? That's collaboration! Witness the transformation of a caterpillar to a butterfly? That's growth!

Wrap up your day by jotting down your observations and what you learned from nature about growth and adaptation. Trust us, nature is one of the best teachers out there!

 So, get your gear ready, pack some snacks, and step out into the great wide open. It's time to embrace the adventurer within you and explore the natural world around you. Here's to an awesome outdoor day!

Day 39: Mindfulness meditation

Okay, today we're going to slow things down a bit. We're jumping into mindfulness meditation. It's going to be cool and chill, promise.

Mindfulness meditation is about focusing on the here and now. Usually, you do this by paying close attention to your breath. Kind of deep, right? But also a great way to relax and let go of any negative energy. Here's the game plan:

1. **Claim your space:** find a quiet spot where you won't be disturbed. Maybe your room, backyard, or a quiet spot at the park. Wear something you feel good in. You can sit on a chair, on the floor, or even lie down.

2. **Watch the clock:** set a timer for 15 minutes. That way, you're not constantly checking your phone.

3. **Eyes shut:** get comfy and close your eyes. The goal is to cut down on distractions. If you're not into closing your eyes, no worries. Just find a fixed point to gaze at.

4. **Follow your breath:** now, focus on your breathing. Feel the air going in and out. Notice your chest or belly rising and falling. Don't try to control your breath, just notice it.

5. **Let your thoughts float by:** if your mind starts to wander off (and it will), that's perfectly okay. When it happens, just notice your thought and then gently bring your focus back to your breath.

6. **Enjoy the quiet:** keep this focus until your timer buzzes. Then, sit quietly for another minute and gently open your eyes.

Now, how do you feel? More relaxed? Clear-headed? It's okay if you're not feeling an instant transformation. The more you meditate, the more you'll notice the effects.

Write down how you felt during and after the meditation in your journal. Remember, meditation is not about clearing your mind completely, it's about being okay with your thoughts. Keep trying, and who knows, you might uncover a whole new level of cool within yourself!

Day 40: Inspirational biographies

Start reading or watching a biography of someone who overcame significant obstacles. Reflect on their growth mindset and how it contributed to their success.

We highly recommend these, but feel free to choose one that you like!

1. *I Am Malala: The Story of the Girl Who Stood Up for Education and Was Shot by the Taliban* by Malala Yousafzai: This powerful autobiography tells the story of Malala, who stood up for education in Pakistan,

despite threats from the Taliban. After surviving an assassination attempt, she went on to become the youngest recipient of the Nobel Peace Prize.

2. *Long Walk to Freedom* by **Nelson Mandela:** Mandela's autobiography recounts his life journey from childhood in a rural village to becoming the first black president of South Africa. His perseverance and unshakeable belief in equality despite being imprisoned for 27 years is a testament to his growth mindset.

3. *The Diary of a Young Girl* by **Anne Frank:** Though not a biography, this diary written by a young girl during the Holocaust, demonstrates remarkable positivity and resilience in the face of unimaginable adversity.

4. *Man's Search for Meaning* by **Viktor E. Frankl:** In this book, psychiatrist Viktor Frankl chronicles his experiences as a prisoner in Nazi concentration camps during World War II and describes his psychotherapeutic method of finding a reason to live. His resilience and mindset of finding purpose in suffering showcases a strong growth mindset.

5. *Steve Jobs* by **Walter Isaacson:** This biography of Steve Jobs, co-founder of Apple Inc, portrays how his belief in his vision and his desire to create world-changing technology drove him to overcome countless obstacles.

Remember, after finishing the biography, reflect on the subject's approach to challenges, how they persevered, and how their growth mindset contributed to their success.

Day 41: Cultivate curiosity

Ask "why" or "how" about something you usually take for granted. Research the answer. How does being curious expand your understanding of the world?

Here are some examples of things we all take for granted. When you think about it, it really is like a miracle!

1. **Social media:** We scroll through feeds without really thinking about the work that goes into creating these platforms. Ask, "how does an algorithm decide what posts to show me?" Or "how is a social media platform built?"

2. **Electricity:** We switch on lights without considering what makes it

possible. Ask, "how does electricity actually get to my house?" Or "how does a light bulb work?"

3. **Cellphones:** We use these devices daily but often overlook the complexity behind their functionality. Ask, "how does my voice convert into a phone call?" Or "how does a touch screen work?"

4. **Music streaming:** We listen to our favorite songs without thinking about the process. Ask, "how does music streaming work?" Or "how do songs get on Spotify or Apple Music?"

5. **Transportation:** We ride in cars or use public transportation without pondering the intricacies. Ask, "how does a car engine work?" Or "what logistics are involved in running a public transit system?"

6. **Food:** We eat meals without understanding the journey our food took to reach us. Ask, "how is this food grown or made?" Or "what's the process of getting food from a farm to my plate?"

7. **Learning:** We go to school and learn without questioning the broader education system. Ask, "how are curriculums decided?" Or "how do different countries approach education?"

By asking "why" or "how," you can begin to understand the complexities and fascinating realities behind everyday experiences, fostering curiosity and a growth mindset.

Day 42: Lend a hand, gain a smile

For today, we're stepping away from our usual routine and stepping into the world of volunteering. Trust me, not only will you be doing a world of good, but you might be surprised at how it can help shift your own mindset. So, here's the game plan:

1. **Choosing your mission:** With so many people and places in need, you've got a ton of options. It could be anything from helping sort food at a local food bank, doing a neighborhood clean-up, or reading books to kiddos at a local library. Pick a cause that feels right for you and get signed up. If there's no event happening immediately, that's okay too. Just commit to doing it in the near future.

2. **The actual doing:** When the day comes, be all in. Participate, contribute,

and absorb the whole experience. Remember, this isn't just about the act of doing good. It's also about learning and growing from the experience.

3. **Thought download:** Once you're done, whip out your trusty journal. Write down your thoughts and feelings about the whole thing. How did volunteering make you feel? Did it change your perspective? Did you notice a shift in your mindset?

Let's imagine you decided to help out at a local food bank. You spent your day sorting donations, packing up meals, and helping distribute them. It might have felt overwhelming at first, right? Like, who knew so many people in your town needed this help?

But as you got stuck in, you might have felt a sense of appreciation wash over you. Seeing the direct effect of your hard work on other people's lives? That's pretty powerful stuff.

In your journal, you could jot down how this experience made you feel more appreciative of what you have, and how meaningful it was to help others. You learned about empathy and the power of community, which has got to be good for the old mindset, right?

Volunteering is more than just a kind act, it's a powerful experience that can help you grow and feel even more connected to the world around you. So, get out there and make a difference!

Day 43: Reflection day

 Reflect on your journey so far. What activities challenged you the most? Which ones made you feel excited or inspired? Keep note of these reflections as you continue your journey.

Remember, cultivating a growth mindset is a marathon, not a sprint. Keep going, and celebrate every bit of progress you make along the way. You're doing an awesome job!

Day 44: Explore your passions day

We all have something that makes our heart race and our eyes light up, right? It could be playing soccer, painting, cooking, or even coding. (And nope, I'm not talking about our shared passion for binge-watching Netflix). Whatever your thing is, today's the day you dive deep into it.

So, here's your task: dedicate a good chunk of today to your passion. If it's soccer, spend time playing, watching, or reading about it. If it's painting, pull out your colors and paint something just for the sheer joy of it. The point is to immerse yourself in something you absolutely love.

Now, while you're having all this fun, I want you to take a moment and really tune into how you feel. Do you feel a surge of energy? A sense of peace, maybe? It's amazing how doing what we love can fuel us and make us feel unstoppable.

But here's the real kicker: your passions aren't just about feeling good. They're also powerful pathways for growth. Notice how when you're engaged in something you're passionate about, you're more willing to take risks, to push your boundaries, and to keep going even when things get tough. You might even discover new areas within your passion that you'd like to learn more about.

That, my friends, is the power of a growth mindset in action! When we're driven by passion, we're more open to learning, exploring, and growing. And guess what? That's something worth celebrating. So go ahead, spend the day doing what you love, and remember: passion and growth go hand in hand!

Day 45: Perfectly imperfect challenge

So, here's your mission for the day: pick an activity—it could be anything from doodling a picture, cooking a meal, to writing a short story—and just go for it without worrying about making it flawless.

Try to embrace the imperfections. If your drawing isn't quite right, or your meal doesn't taste like something that came out of Gordon Ramsey's kitchen, that's okay! If your story doesn't sound like it's fresh off the New York Times bestseller list, no worries!

While you're at it, take some time to reflect. How does it feel to let go of the idea of perfection? Is it freeing? Uncomfortable? Maybe a little bit of both? That's perfectly fine. Remember, growth happens when we step out of our comfort zones.

Also, pay attention to what you can learn from this experience. Maybe you discover a new way of drawing, a new flavor combination in your cooking, or a fresh idea for your story. In the pursuit of perfection, these discoveries might have been overlooked.

This challenge is a cool way to remind ourselves that it's okay not to be perfect. What really matters is that we're trying, learning, and growing. Perfection might be a cool concept, but remember, it's our perfectly imperfect efforts that lead to real growth and learning.

Day 46: Step into the Ted Talk zone

Alright team, get ready for a new type of mission. Today, we're trading in the pen and paper for a screen and speakers. We're diving into the world of Ted Talks, where we'll get to hear from the best of the best, people who've spent their lives exploring the growth mindset.

Ted Talks are like a global stage for great ideas. And lucky for us, there are a ton of these talks all about the growth mindset. Today, your job is to pick one, give it a watch, and take a moment to reflect on what you've learned. It's like having a personal lecture from some of the world's greatest thinkers—right from your own living room!

Here are a few options to kick off your search:

1. **"The Power Of Believing That You Can Improve"** by Carol Dweck

2. **"Grit: The Power of Passion and Perseverance"** by Angela Lee Duckworth

3. **"How to Get Better at the Things You Care About"** by Eduardo Briceño

These are just to get you started. Feel free to venture off into the vast world of Ted Talks and find a gem that really speaks to you. After you've watched your talk, give yourself a bit of time to mull it over. Ask yourself:

1. Which idea or message from the talk really stood out to you?

2. How does what you heard connect to your understanding of the growth mindset?

3. Can you think of ways to bring the speaker's insights into your own journey?

This isn't some boring assignment, it's a chance to see what's happening at the forefront of growth mindset thinking. So settle in, pop some popcorn, and get ready to learn something amazing.

Remember, growth isn't a sprint—it's a lifelong journey. So take a deep breath, hit play, and get ready to see where this ted talk takes you!

Day 47: Create a vision board-design your dreams

Today, we're putting on our creative hats and crafting a vision board! If you're thinking "wait, what's a vision board?," hold tight, I've got you covered. A vision board is basically a vibrant collage of pictures, phrases, and items that symbolize your dreams, goals, and all the awesome stuff you want to achieve.

This isn't just about making a snazzy poster to jazz up your wall. It's about creating a visual roadmap of your future, a reminder of where you're headed and the fantastic journey that awaits. They say a picture is worth a thousand words, right? So, let's harness the power of imagery.

Here's your mission for the day:

1. **Get your gear ready:** hunt down a big piece of paper or cardboard, some magazines, printed images, markers, scissors, and glue. If you're more into tech, you can design your vision board online with tools like Canva.

2. **Picture your goals:** take a moment to really mull over your dreams and goals. When you imagine your future, what do you see? Which words encapsulate what you want to achieve?

3. **Hunt for images:** this part's super fun! Dive into your magazines or surf the web for pictures that mirror your goals and the steps needed to get there. The images should resonate with you, and spark a sense of joy and motivation.

4. **Assemble your masterpiece:** start sticking your images and words onto your board. Don't worry about getting it perfect—it's your board, your vision, so let it reflect you.

5. **Position your vision board:** once you've got your board just how you want it, place it somewhere you'll see daily. This is your daily shot of inspiration and motivation!

For example, if you're dreaming of becoming a musician, your board might have pictures of your music idols, images of instruments, concert stages, a collage of music notes, and words like 'determination,' 'passion,' and 'practice.'

Seeing this each day will keep your goal fresh in your mind and remind you of the growth mindset needed to reach it.

Enjoy this activity, put your unique spin on it, and let your creativity flow. Crafting a vision board is like sketching your dreams on a canvas. It's empowering, thrilling, and serves as a visual nudge of the exciting journey you've embarked on. Time to get your craft on!

Day 48: Skill up–your next adventure

Ready for a new adventure today? We're about to pick up a new skill. Now, before you start worrying about being perfect right off the bat, drop that thought. This isn't about nailing it instantly. Remember, it's all about progress, not perfection.

So, here's your challenge for today:

1. **Choose your skill:** this could be anything you've been wanting to learn. Maybe you've always wanted to strum a guitar, solve a Rubik's Cube, or whip up a tasty homemade pizza from scratch.

2. **Find your guide:** look up resources that can help you get started. This could be YouTube tutorials, online courses, or how-to books. For example, if you're picking up a guitar for the first time, there are loads of beginner tutorials online that break down the basics into easy steps.

3. **Dive in:** start your learning journey. Spend some time today diving into your new skill. Remember, you're just starting out, so don't fret about any initial hiccups.

4. **Reflect:** at the end of your first day of learning, take a moment to reflect on how it went. What was challenging? What was exciting? What did you learn about yourself in the process?

For instance, let's say you decided to learn how to solve a Rubik's Cube. Your first step would be finding a beginner's guide or tutorial. Then, you'd spend some time familiarizing yourself with the cube and the initial steps to solve it. At first, it may feel tricky and confusing. But remember, every master was once a beginner. The point isn't to solve the cube today, it's to start the process and enjoy the learning journey.

This new skill adventure is a fantastic way to exercise your growth mindset.

As you learn and improve over time, you'll see firsthand how persistence, curiosity, and a positive attitude towards challenges can lead to growth. So, what's the new skill you're going to conquer?

Day 49: DIY day-gear up for discovery

It's time to tap into that overflowing creativity of yours. You've been strengthening your growth mindset muscles throughout this journey and now, it's time to put them to the test.

What's on the agenda? A DIY (do it yourself) project. The kicker? It's got to be something you've never done before. Scary? Maybe a little. Exciting? Absolutely!

DIY projects aren't just about creating something out of nothing. They're a direct line to your problem-solving prowess. Every step in a DIY project is a challenge to face, a hurdle to leap over. They're miniature growth mindset boot camps, so to speak.

So here's what you need to do:

CHALLENGE: BUILD, CREATE, GROW!

1. **Pick your project:** it's got to be something new. Something that makes you say, "can I really do this?" That's your sweet spot.

2. **Make a plan:** what are the steps you need to take to finish this project? Sketch it out. Planning is key.

3. **Get your gear:** gather all the resources you need. Everything from duct tape to YouTube tutorials, have it handy.

4. **Go for it:** dive headfirst into your project. Remember, perfection isn't the goal here. Learning and evolving are.

5. **Reflect:** after you've completed your project, take a step back. What did you learn from this? What would you do differently next time?

So there it is. Your next adventure. A brand new skill waiting to be explored. Get ready to discover more about yourself and remember, the main aim is to enjoy the process.

Day 50: Reflect and celebrate!

Whoa, hold up, did we just reach Day 50? You bet we did! And that, my friends, is an achievement worth celebrating. You've stuck to this journey like a champ, but remember, the best part isn't just getting here, but the mind-boggling growth that you've journeyed through. So, today is about two super cool things—reliving the ride we've been on, and toasting to our epic wins.

1. **Memory lane:** let's press the rewind button and look back at the past 50 days. What were the moments that made you say "Wow!"? What were the bumps along the road? Did you grow in ways that caught you by surprise? Jot these down in your journal, or better yet, chat about it with your buddies or family. You've been building up your growth mindset, learning all sorts of new stuff, confronting fears, turning failures on their heads, and so much more. Recognizing how far you've come is like adding rocket fuel to your growth journey.

2. **Party time:** now comes the fun part—time to break out the confetti for each step you took, each hurdle you cleared, and every bit of progress you made. And hey, don't just look at the giant leaps. Even the baby steps count. That time when you chose to learn from a slip-up or that day when you decided to push through even when things got tough? Yep, they're worth a victory dance!

3. **Eyes on the horizon:** lastly, let's think about what lies ahead. What are some things you're keen to keep working on? Are there new challenges that you're itching to tackle? Remember, growing your mindset isn't a one-time event, it's a never-ending adventure.

Take a moment to reflect on this journey, the challenges you overcame, and how you've grown in the process. Celebrate these wins—from picking up a new skill to sticking to your practice, to confronting your fears. And as you look ahead, maybe you decide to keep rocking the guitar or try your hand at another instrument.

This isn't the end of the road, it's just the start of your epic growth mindset journey. But today, go ahead and give yourself a big thumbs up, crank up your favorite tunes, and indulge in your favorite treat—you've absolutely earned it! And remember, you've taken a huge leap toward becoming an even more awesome version of you. Hats off to you, and here's to keeping the growth going!

CHAPTER 11

Essential Tips to Keep the Growth Mindset Momentum Going

You've shown incredible dedication during the past 50-Day Challenge, and we bet you're feeling the impact of all that hard work. And that's why we don't want this to be just a fleeting experiment but a permanent way of life. So, how do we make sure we don't lose that brilliant momentum?

We're so glad you asked.

Because we've got some turbo-charged tools in store for you in this chapter. These tools will keep your growth mindset engine running, no matter what obstacles you face or how far away your goals might seem.

In this chapter, we'll dig deeper into each of these tools, learn why they're so awesome for keeping the growth mindset momentum alive, and how you can use them every single day. Ready to jump right in? Awesome, because first up, we're taking a deep dive into the powerful world of visualization.

Power of visualization: seeing is believing

Let's dive into something straight-up magical: visualization. You might be thinking, "isn't that just fancy daydreaming?" Nope, not at all. Visualization is like drawing up a mental picture or a movie about your goals, and more importantly, you winning at them. And the neat thing about it? It's a brain hack!

So here's the deal: your brain isn't too sharp at telling the difference between what's real and what's imagined. So, when you visualize crushing your goals, your brain is getting a taste of success, and it starts believing that it's all achievable. It's like tricking your brain into growth mode!

Alright, enough with the chit-chat. Let's try this out!

Your imagination = your superpower

Let's kick things off with a simple exercise to get those visualization muscles working.

Find a comfy spot, close your eyes, and take a deep breath. Picture yourself battling a super tough task, something that seems way out of your league right now. See yourself breaking it down into bite-sized pieces, working on each bit, learning, and getting better.

Imagine that moment when you totally get it. When you've conquered it. Can you feel the surge of accomplishment? That's what we're talking about. Open your eyes and hold on to that feeling.

That right there? That's what growth feels like, and it's waiting for you to grab it.

Visualization: your new daily ritual

Now you're probably thinking, "yeah, this is cool, but how do I do this every day?" We've got you covered. Here are a few tips to help you get visualization into your daily grind:

Make it a routine: like any other habit, you gotta stick with visualization. Pick a time each day that works for you—maybe when you wake up or before you go to sleep—and dedicate it to your visualization practice.

Start with baby steps: no need to imagine you're winning a Nobel Prize right off the bat. Start with small, reachable goals, and then go bigger.

Bring on the feels: the more feelings you can bring into your visualization, the better it'll work. Really try to feel what it's like to achieve your goal.

Stay positive: keep your visualizations bright and sunny. This helps boost your confidence and gets you into a growth mindset.

Remember, it might feel a bit odd at first, but keep at it and soon it'll feel as natural as breathing. Keep it up, and watch your growth mindset skyrocket!

Express yourself: journaling your way to growth

Now, let's switch gears and talk about another fantastic tool in your growth mindset toolbox: journaling. You may be wondering, "isn't journaling just for my little cousin who keeps a diary about her pet hamster?" Not quite, my friend. Journaling is a powerful tool for self-discovery, and it's a fantastic way to foster your growth mindset. Here's how.

Why journal? What's the point?

Imagine journaling as a mirror. But not the regular kind that just shows your epic bed hair in the morning. No, this is a mirror for your thoughts, your feelings, your hopes, and your challenges. It's a space where you can be 100% you, with no filters, no judgments.

Journaling helps you get all those jumbled thoughts out of your head and onto paper. It can help you identify patterns and triggers in your thoughts. More importantly, it allows you to reflect on your growth and progress. And hey, it's a scientifically proven fact that writing down your thoughts and feelings can help reduce stress and anxiety. So there's that.

And let's not forget, you've been keeping a journal throughout this 50-day growth mindset challenge. You've seen how powerful it can be to record and reflect on your journey. So, why not keep the momentum going?

Prompts to propel you forward

Not sure what to write? No worries. Let's kickstart your journaling journey with some daily prompts designed to help you embrace your growth mindset:

1. What's one challenge you faced today? How did you handle it, and what could you do differently next time?

2. Write about a time when you made a mistake. What did you learn from it?

3. What's something new you'd like to learn, and why? What's the first step you could take toward it?

4. What's a recent accomplishment you're proud of? Celebrate it in writing!

5. Write a letter to your future self, expressing your hopes and what you want to have learned or achieved.

Remember, there's no right or wrong answer. Just let your thoughts flow freely.

Making journaling a habit

Journaling can be as flexible as you want it to be. You can write every day, or just when you feel like it. You can write a novel's worth, or just jot down bullet points. The key is to make it work for you. So grab a notebook (or start a new document on your computer, or a note on your phone), get comfy, and start writing.

Like with visualization, make journaling a part of your routine. Maybe it's the first thing you do in the morning to set the tone for your day. Or perhaps it's your evening wind-down activity. Just find your rhythm and stick with it.

And there you have it! Journaling, another tool for your growth mindset arsenal. Give it a try, and don't forget to enjoy the journey of self-discovery and growth it will surely lead you on!

Speak it into existence: positive affirmations for growth

 Ever heard the saying, "fake it 'til you make it?" Turns out, there's some truth to it. But, we're not talking about faking skills or knowledge. Nope. We're talking about faking confidence, positivity, and resilience until it's not faking anymore. It becomes who you are. That's where positive affirmations come into play.

Affirmations: your personal cheerleader

Let's be real. We all have those days when nothing seems to go right. You mess up that math problem, trip over your shoelaces, or just feel kind of blah. It's easy to let those days dictate how you feel about yourself. But here's the kicker: they don't have to. That's where affirmations come in.

Affirmations are positive statements that you repeat to yourself. They're like your own personal cheerleader, always there to boost your spirits. And guess what? They can actually help rewire your brain to believe what you're saying. So, if you keep telling yourself, "I am capable of learning and growing," guess what? Your brain starts to believe it.

Amp up your growth with these affirmations

Ready to get started with affirmations? Great! Here are a few examples to help kickstart your growth mindset:

1. "I embrace challenges as opportunities to learn and grow."

2. "Mistakes are part of my learning process."

3. "I am becoming better each day."

4. "I have the power to control my thoughts and reactions."

5. "Every setback is a setup for a comeback."

Feel free to use these, tweak them, or come up with your own. The key is to find affirmations that resonate with you.

Craft your own cheerleader chants

Now that you've got a feel for it, why not try crafting your own affirmations? It's like creating a custom-made cheerleader chant, specifically designed for you. Here's a little how-to:

1. **Keep it positive.** Your affirmation should be an encouraging note to yourself, not a put-down.

2. **Make it present tense.** Instead of saying, "I will be good at this," say, "I am good at this." It's about believing you have the power right now.

3. **Be specific.** General affirmations are great, but sometimes being specific gives that extra oomph.

You've just created your own personal cheerleader. Remember, the more you repeat your affirmations, the more you'll start to believe them. So make it a daily habit, and watch your growth mindset blossom.

Here's the deal, squad. Developing a growth mindset isn't a one-and-done kind of deal. It's not like flipping a switch and, poof, you're suddenly all about growth and positivity. It's more like mastering a new dance move, hitting a new high score in a video game, or nailing a complex skate trick. You get the idea. It takes practice, time, and a heap of patience.

Just like how every line of code matters in a complex software, or every ingredient matters in a recipe, every moment you spend fostering your growth mindset counts. It's not about perfection but persistence. Every time you choose to challenge yourself, embrace failure as a stepping stone, or swap out a "can't" with a "can't yet," you're flexing those growth mindset muscles. The more you flex, the stronger they get.

Remember, our 50-day program is here to help you on this journey. It's got your back, and it's brimming with exercises, activities, and insights to help you nurture your growth mindset. Stick with it. Consistency is key.

Remember that super-hard video game level that took forever to beat? You know the one. You tried again and again, maybe even rage quit a couple of times. But, eventually, you figured it out. You learned from each failed attempt, and when you finally nailed it, the victory was sweet.

Your growth mindset journey is a lot like that. It's going to have its tough moments and times where you feel like you're not getting anywhere. That's totally okay. It's all part of the process. Embrace it.

The goal here isn't to eliminate struggle or to always be positive. It's to understand that struggle is part of learning, and it's through challenges that we grow.

So don't sweat the downs. They're just as important as the ups.

CHAPTER 12

A Parent's Guide to a Growth Mindset

Being a parent to a teen is a wild, exciting, and sometimes baffling ride, wouldn't you agree? You're not just a driver's ed instructor, homework helper, or the "because I said so" voice of reason. You're also a huge influence on how your teenager sees the world, including how they perceive their own abilities and potential. Yeah, no pressure, right?

But before you panic, know this: your role in your teen's development is not about being perfect. It's about guiding them to be the best version of themselves. It's like being a gardener, giving the right amount of sunlight, water, and nutrients to help the plant—or in this case, your teen—grow.

And this is where the concept of a growth mindset comes in. If you're unfamiliar, don't worry, we've got your back! Simply put, a growth mindset is all about believing that our abilities can develop over time. It's about looking at challenges and setbacks as opportunities to grow and learn, rather than seeing them as impenetrable brick walls.

Sounds pretty empowering, doesn't it? Well, it's not just a feel-good concept. Research shows that nurturing a growth mindset in your teenager can have a whole bunch of benefits. It can boost their self-esteem, increase resilience, and even improve academic performance. It's like giving them a tool to navigate life's ups, downs, twists, and turns.

In the pages that follow, we'll delve deeper into how you—as a parent—can encourage and support this mindset in your teenager. It's an incredible journey you're about to embark on, so let's get going!

Encouraging a growth mindset in your teenager

Okay, so we've covered the basics of what a growth mindset is and why it's important. Now let's talk about how to actually encourage this in your teen. Don't fret, we're not about to suggest anything wild like making them climb Mount Everest or write the next 'War and Peace'. It's all about small, doable actions that create a big impact.

Firstly, start recognizing effort over results. Yeah, an A on the test is great, but what about the hours of studying? What about the tenacity shown when a tough problem was tackled and eventually solved? Those deserve some serious appreciation too. By shifting your focus to the process—the effort, strategies, and determination—you'll help your teen see that hard work, not just natural talent or smarts, is a big part of success.

Secondly, be a role model of a growth mindset. It's one thing to tell your teen that mistakes are opportunities to learn, and quite another to show them.

CREATE A GROWTH-FRIENDLY HOME:
4 SIMPLE STEPS

CREATE A SPACE WHERE FAILURE IS SEEN AS PART OF LEARNING, NOT SOMETHING TO AVOID

REFLECT DAILY ON EFFORT AND IMPROVEMENTS MADE THROUGHOUT THE DAY

ENCOURAGE FAMILY DISCUSSIONS ABOUT CHALLENGES AND WHAT EVERYONE LEARNED

ASK GROWTH-FOCUSED QUESTIONS AT DINNER LIKE, "WHAT WAS THE BIGGEST CHALLENGE TODAY, AND HOW DID YOU FACE IT?"

Don't shy away from your own goof-ups. Acknowledge them, laugh about them, and most importantly, show your teen how you learn from them.

But what about practical exercises? Good question! Here's a simple one: next time your teen is faced with a challenging task, ask them to list down the skills they need to complete it. Then, help them come up with a plan to develop these skills. It's all about breaking down the task into manageable parts and tackling each one step by step.

Finally, consider the environment at home. Is it okay to make mistakes? Is curiosity encouraged? Try to create a space where questions, creativity, and yes, even failure are welcomed. It could be as simple as asking "what did you learn today?" Instead of "did you win or lose?" At the dinner table.

Remember, encouraging a growth mindset isn't a one-time event. It's a continuous process that happens bit by bit, day by day. It may seem like you're not making much headway at first, but trust us, every little bit counts. So go ahead, and start planting those seeds of growth.

Supporting your teenager's growth journey

We get it. Being a parent is tough work, especially when you've got a teenager in the mix. There's a lot of emotion, a ton of change, and an endless list of challenges. But here's the deal: your role in this phase of their life is crucial, and your support is irreplaceable.

Emotional support and guidance go a long way. And we're not just talking about a pat on the back or a 'good job' here and there. Genuine support is about being there, listening, and understanding—even when things get messy. And trust us, with teens, things can get very messy. You can't fix everything, and that's alright. Sometimes, the best support you can give is to simply sit with them in their mess until they're ready to clean it up.

Now let's talk about resilience and perseverance. Life is not all sunshine and rainbows, and it's important that your teen understands that. But more than that, it's crucial they know they can weather the storm. When they come across a challenge or a setback, help them view it as just another puzzle to be solved, not an insurmountable wall. Encourage them to try different approaches, to keep going even when things are tough. And remind them—progress, not perfection, is the goal.

Speaking of setbacks, they're inevitable. Everyone trips up at some point. But here's the thing: it's not the falling down that matters, it's the getting back up. Teach your teen that mistakes are not catastrophes, but learning opportunities. When they stumble, help them analyze what went wrong and how they can improve next time. Instead of hiding failures under the rug, put them in the spotlight and explore them. It may feel uncomfortable at first, but this is how growth happens.

Supporting your teen's growth journey may seem like a daunting task. And to be honest, it can be. But remember, you're not alone in this. Reach out, seek advice and share experiences. Your support can make a world of difference to your teen. So be there, be present, and watch them grow.

The power of conversation: talking about growth mindset

Alright, parents, here's the deal: talking about a growth mindset isn't like solving a math equation. There's no definite solution, no exact formula. It's a dance—a combination of listening, understanding, asking, and discussing. Sounds challenging, right? But don't worry, we've got you covered.

Conversations about growth mindset shouldn't feel like a lecture. You're not there to tell them what to think or do, but to guide them towards understanding their potential for growth. To get this dance started, try to weave in growth mindset concepts into everyday chats. Talk about your own experiences with a growth mindset, or bring up stories of people who've shown a growth mindset in their lives.

But what if your teen isn't all that keen on chatting? We hear you. Teens can be a tough crowd to crack. Here's where conversation starters can come in handy. Think of them like secret conversation keys—just the right thing to unlock that dialogue door.

Here are some questions to help you get the growth mindset conversations started with your teens:

1. "I noticed you worked really hard on that project, even when it was challenging. How did you keep yourself motivated?"

2. "Was there ever a time when you had to change your strategy to succeed in something? What did you learn from that experience?"

3. "Can you think of a time when you saw someone else demonstrate a growth mindset? How did it inspire you?"

4. "What's something challenging that you've always wanted to try? Let's brainstorm some first steps together."

5. "If you could learn a new skill right now, what would it be and why? What's stopping you from starting?"

6. "I remember a time when I faced a difficult situation. Do you want to hear about it?"

7. "Have you ever felt like you just couldn't do something, but then you managed to do it after all? How did that make you feel?"

8. "Do you think a person's intelligence and abilities are set in stone or can they change over time? Why do you think so?"

9. "Who's a person you admire for their determination and perseverance? What can we learn from them?"

Remember, these are starters—the goal is to get the conversation going, but let it flow naturally from there. Listen to their responses and continue the discussion based on what they say.

Now, we know how much you love your kids and want to see them grow. **But remember, it's not all about the praise. It's about the feedback.** Not the kind that tears them down, but the kind that builds them up—the constructive kind. When providing feedback, focus on their effort and strategies rather than the outcome. Saying something like, "you put a lot of effort into that project, and it shows!" Can be much more beneficial than just saying, "great job!"

Talking about a growth mindset is like planting seeds. You might not see results straight away, but with patience, care, and a whole lot of conversation, you'll soon see those growth mindset plants start to sprout. So, get talking, and watch the magic happen.

YOU PUT IN A LOT OF EFFORT AND IT SHOWS!

Navigating challenges: dealing with resistance and fixed mindset traps

Alright, let's get real for a moment. No journey is smooth sailing, and the journey to a growth mindset is no different. There will be moments of resistance, setbacks, and even times when your teen might fall into a fixed mindset trap. And that's okay! After all, we're human, and we're not striving for perfection here, but growth.

So how can you spot a fixed mindset in your teen? Well, it's all about language and behavior. Maybe they say things like, "I'm just not good at this," or they give up quickly when they face a challenging task. That's the fixed mindset talking.

When you spot these fixed mindset moments, help your teen flip the script. Encourage them to see these moments as opportunities for growth, not failure. If they say, "I can't do this," guide them to add the powerful word 'yet' at the end. "I can't do this yet." See, it changes everything!

Now, we've got to address the elephant in the room—your own mindset. Yes, you! Parents can fall into fixed mindset traps too. It's important to model a growth mindset because your actions often speak louder than words. **You might feel the urge to step in and fix things when your teen is struggling, but hold back. Show them that it's okay to struggle, it's okay to fail, and it's okay to ask for help.**

By dealing with your own fixed mindset tendencies and helping your teen overcome theirs, you're not just nurturing a growth mindset. There's a plethora of books, videos, and documentaries on the subject that could help you learn more about the growth mindset! We've curated a list of our favorites down in Resources and Bibliography, so be sure to check them out.

 You're also building resilience, promoting self-confidence, and fostering a love for learning.

Collaborating with schools and teachers

You're not in this alone. As much as you're a major player in your teen's life, there are other key characters in this growth mindset story. Yes, we're talking about schools and teachers. They spend a significant amount of time with your teen and can be strong allies on this growth journey.

Education plays a massive role in shaping a teen's mindset. Classrooms can either nourish a growth mindset or feed a fixed one, depending on how they are structured. Lessons, assignments, and even assessments can be designed to highlight the power of effort, persistence, and learning from mistakes. That's why it's essential to get to know the environment your teen is learning in.

You might be wondering, "Okay, but how do I do that?" Start by building a solid relationship with your teen's teachers. It's about communication, understanding, and collaboration. Share your goals for fostering a growth mindset in your teen. Ask the teachers about their teaching strategies, how they give feedback, and how they handle mistakes and failures in the classroom.

Next, you could also suggest activities or programs that promote a growth mindset. These can be as simple as a "Mistake of the Week" where students share a mistake they made and what they learned from it, or a "growth mindset award" for students who've shown remarkable effort and resilience. If your school is open to it, you could even propose workshops or seminars for students, teachers, and even other parents about the growth mindset.

Fostering a growth mindset in your teen isn't just a home project—it's a community effort. Schools, teachers, and even classmates have a role to play. When you all work together, you're setting the stage for not just your teen, but every student, to embrace the power of growth.

Here's what you need to remember: you're playing the long game. Every little step you take, every conversation, every instance where you choose to encourage effort over results, you're slowly but surely influencing your teen's mindset. It's like planting a seed and watching it grow. Sure, you might not see changes immediately, but given time and the right conditions, that tiny seed can grow into a sturdy, resilient tree.

And finally, let's not forget why we're doing all of this. A growth mindset isn't just some trend. It's a way of living that can profoundly impact your teen's life. From how they face challenges, and how they view their abilities, to how they deal with setbacks, a growth mindset can be a powerful tool for them to navigate through the winding road of life. It's not about creating overachievers; it's about nurturing resilient, adaptable, and lifelong learners.

Before We Wrap Up!

We're stoked that you've journeyed with us through *The Essential Growth Mindset Handbook for Teens*. We hope you're feeling more empowered to embrace challenges, persist in the face of setbacks, and understand that effort is the path to mastery. If you've found the book helpful, we'd be super grateful if you could share your thoughts with us.

Your feedback is not just super important to us, but it's also a gift to other teens, parents, and educators who are searching for ways to cultivate a growth mindset. When you leave a review, you're essentially helping others kickstart their own mindset revolution. And that's a pretty awesome thing to do!

Think of writing a review as your final challenge in this handbook—a test of your growth mindset. Faced with this challenge, remember, you're more than capable of acing it. By sharing your experiences, you're embracing the opportunity to grow and also helping others do the same.

We really appreciate your time and your contribution. Together, we're helping to encourage and inspire a new generation of growth mindset champions.

Scan this QR code to leave a quick 1-minute review!

Your feedback is mega valuable, not just for us, but also for other teens, parents, and educators who are navigating the journey to a growth mindset. Your insights contribute to the growth and evolution of RaiseYouthRight. We're on a mission to make the next generation more resilient, flexible, and mentally stronger, and your contribution gets us one step closer!

Thanks again for being part of our growth mindset community. Remember, growth is a lifelong journey, so keep embracing challenges, keep persisting, and most of all, keep growing!

Conclusion

Let's drop some truth right here! A growth mindset isn't a fad or a trend that'll disappear like yesterday's viral TikTok dance. Nope, it's here to stay because it brings about some real positive changes, not just in your day-to-day grind, but throughout your whole life. You see, the rad part of having a growth mindset is that it allows you to keep learning, keep growing, and stay curious. It encourages you to look at challenges, stumble, then dust off and rise again, stronger than before.

You've come this far, why stop now? Remember, the journey of growth doesn't end when you close this book or after a 50-Day Program, it's a lifelong adventure. You might be thinking, "wow, lifelong? That's a long time." But hey, once you start seeing the perks, you won't want to go back.

The journey may be full of ups and downs, sure, but it's worth it. Think of it as your favorite song, you know, the one that starts slow, builds up, and then drops the beat making you want to jump and dance. The journey of growth is like that, exciting and unpredictable, but oh-so satisfying. So, keep that energy going, and remember that your attitude determines your direction.

To keep you pumped up, think about the countless individuals out there who've embraced a growth mindset and have seen their lives transformed. People like you and me, who took charge of their lives, are committed to our growth and have witnessed mind-blowing results. They're not just stories. They are real experiences. From acing that challenging math exam to nailing the guitar solo, from leading a school project to overcoming a fear of public speaking—the victories are endless!

So go forth and embrace the beautiful journey of growth and remember, you're never alone in this. We're all in this together, growing, learning, and evolving, one day at a time.

Life isn't a race to the finish line, but a journey of growth to be savored every step of the way.

Resources and Bibliography

Chapter 2: Understanding the Teenage Brain

Answer key to quiz

The brainy word unscramble
Brain, amygdala, neuroplasticity

The brainy crossword
Across

2—Dopamine

5—Neuroplasticity

6—Prefrontal cortex

Down

1—Adolescence

3—Growth mindset

4—Hippocampus

7—Amygdala

The 'what comes next' challenge
Pattern 1: 33 (each number adds the multiple of 3 from the previous one.)

Pattern 2: 44 (each number adds the multiple of 4 from the previous one.)

Pattern 3: 55 (each number adds the multiple of 5 from the previous one.)

Pattern 4: 240 (each number is quadrupled from the previous one.)

Pattern 5: 14348907 (each number is the square of the previous one.)

Pattern 6: 2384185791015625 (each number is the square of the previous one.)

Brainy riddles

Riddle 1: an echo

Riddle 2: the letter 'e'

Riddle 3: a map

Riddle 4: footsteps

Riddle 5: pencil lead

Riddle 6: a cloud

Riddle 7: a promise

Riddle 8: your breath

Riddle 9: a piano

Riddle 10: fire

Smart goals template

Feel free to download and print it out using this link right here!

Combined resource list

Books

1. *Mindset: The New Psychology of Success* by Carol S. Dweck—Dweck's exploration of the "fixed" and "growth" mindsets can help teens and parents understand the power of believing in one's capacity for growth and development.

2. *Grit: The Power of Passion and Perseverance* by Angela Duckworth—This book emphasizes the importance of resilience and perseverance over pure talent, inspiring teens to stay determined in their pursuits.

3. *Make It Stick: The Science of Successful Learning* by Peter C. Brown— Provides insights into effective learning strategies that can help teens maximize their academic potential.

4. *Daring Greatly: How the Courage to Be Vulnerable Transforms the Way We Live, Love, Parent, and Lead* by Brene Brown—Promotes emotional openness and vulnerability, critical for healthy communication between parents and teens.

6. *The Champion's Mind: How Great Athletes Think, Train, and Thrive* by Jim Afremow—Offers inspiration to teens from the perspective of successful athletes, teaching them about discipline, perseverance, and mental strength.

7. *The Inner Game of Tennis: The Classic Guide to the Mental Side of Peak Performance* by W. Timothy Gallwey—The mental strategies in this book can help teens optimize their performance in various fields, not just sports.

8. *The Power of Full Engagement: Managing Energy, Not Time, Is the Key to High Performance and Personal Renewal* by Jim Loehr & Tony Schwartz— Teaches teens and parents about energy management, which can lead to improved performance and well-being.

9. *Measure What Matters: How Google, Bono, and the Gates Foundation Rock the World with OKRs* by John Doerr—Highlights the power of setting and tracking objectives and key results (OKRs), a practice applicable to academic and personal growth goals.

10. *Smarter Faster Better: The Secrets of Being Productive in Life and Business* by Charles Duhigg—Outlines productivity techniques that can assist teens in achieving their goals more efficiently.

11. *The Desire Map: A Guide to Creating Goals with Soul* by Danielle LaPorte— Guides readers in setting heartfelt, meaningful goals, helping teens connect more deeply with their ambitions.

12. *The Growth Mindset Coach: A Teacher's Month-by-Month Handbook for Empowering Students to Achieve* by Annie Brock and Heather Hundley—

Provides educators and parents with strategies to foster a growth mindset in students.

13. *Parenting Teens With Love And Logic: Preparing Adolescents for Responsible Adulthood* by Charles Fay and Foster Cline—Gives parents effective techniques to guide their teens toward becoming responsible adults.

14. *The Growth Mindset Playbook: A Teacher's Guide to Promoting Student Success* by Annie Brock and Heather Hundley—A practical guide for educators and parents to support student success through growth mindset principles.

15. *The Whole-Brain Child: 12 Revolutionary Strategies to Nurture Your Child's Developing Mind* by Daniel J. Siegel and Tina Payne Bryson—Offers neuroscience-backed strategies to nurture children's emotional and intellectual development.

16. *"Raising Resilient Children: Fostering Strength, Hope, and Optimism in Your Child* by Robert Brooks and Sam Goldstein—Provides guidance on raising children to be resilient, a critical aspect of the growth mindset.

17. *Mindsets for Parents: Strategies to Encourage Growth Mindsets in Kids* by Mary Cay Ricci and Margaret Lee—Delivers practical strategies for parents to nurture a growth mindset in their children, fostering resilience and a love for learning in their teen years.

18. *UnSelfie: Why Empathetic Kids Succeed in Our All-About-Me World* by Michele Borba—Advocates for the cultivation of empathy in children, a critical skill for effective communication and relationship-building in adulthood.

19. *How Children Succeed: Grit, Curiosity, and the Hidden Power of Character* by Paul Tough—Highlights the significance of character traits like grit and curiosity over intelligence in determining success, inspiring parents and teens to prioritize these attributes.

20. *How to Raise an Adult: Break Free of the Overparenting Trap and Prepare Your Kid for Success* by Julie Lythcott-Haims—Encourages parents to allow their teens more autonomy, helping them develop essential life skills and self-efficacy.

21. *No-Drama Discipline: The Whole-Brain Way to Calm the Chaos and Nurture*

Your Child's Developing Mind by Daniel J. Siegel and Tina Payne Bryson—Outlines compassionate, drama-free discipline strategies that foster a nurturing parent-child relationship.

22. *Drive: The Surprising Truth About What Motivates Us* by Daniel H. Pink—Delves into the psychology of motivation, aiding parents and teens in understanding what truly drives success and fulfillment

TED Talks and videos

Carol Dweck: The Power of Believing You Can Improve
Psychologist Carol Dweck introduces her research on "mindsets" and demonstrates how believing in our ability to improve, the growth mindset, can drastically change our approach to learning and personal development.

Eduardo Briceño: The Power of Belief—Mindset and Success
The co-founder of Mindset Works, Briceño elaborates on the difference between a growth mindset and a fixed mindset, and how our perceptions of our abilities can influence our success.

Rita Pierson: Every Kid Needs a Champion
Veteran educator Pierson underscores the significance of relationships and connections in education, advocating for teachers and mentors who genuinely believe in their students' potential for growth.

Angela Lee Duckworth: Grit: The Power of Passion and Perseverance
Duckworth, a psychologist, shares her findings on how "grit"—a blend of passion and long-term perseverance—plays a crucial role in achieving success, more than conventional factors like IQ or family income.

Brene Brown: The Power of Vulnerability
Brene Brown, a research professor, shares her research on human connection and the importance of vulnerability in building relationships and cultivating self-acceptance, a key aspect of personal growth.

Guy Winch: Why We All Need to Practice Emotional First Aid
Psychologist Guy Winch makes a compelling case for prioritizing emotional health, teaching us how to handle common emotional injuries such as rejection and failure, which are inevitable on the path of growth.

Carol Dweck: The Power of Yet

In this talk, Dweck expands on her growth mindset concept, focusing on the power of "yet"—a word that signifies a journey towards improvement and opens the door to possibilities.

Kobe Bryant's Last Great Interview

In his last significant interview, basketball legend Kobe Bryant delves into his mentality towards life and sports, exhibiting how a growth mindset helped him become one of the greatest athletes of his time.

Sal Khan: Let's teach for mastery, not test scores

This talk emphasizes the importance of focusing on mastery of knowledge and skills rather than purely on test scores, promoting the idea of growth and learning at one's own pace.

David Yeager: Growth Mindset, Belonging, and Purpose

Yeager discusses the impact of social and psychological factors on academic achievement, exploring how growth mindset can be fostered in educational settings.

Linda Cliatt-Wayman: How to fix a broken school? Lead fearlessly, love hard

As a principal of a troubled Philadelphia high school, Cliatt-Wayman shares her experiences in implementing change and fostering a culture of success, encapsulating the essence of the growth mindset.

Johann Hari: This could be why you're depressed or anxious

While primarily a talk on mental health, this TED Talk can aid in understanding some of the underlying psychological aspects that may influence the adoption of a growth or fixed mindset.

Movies and documentaries

Movies

The Pursuit of Happyness

This biographical drama film portrays the true story of Chris Gardner, a struggling salesman who becomes homeless with his young son, but never gives up, ultimately becoming a successful stockbroker.

Wonder

A heartwarming story of a child with Treacher Collins syndrome. The movie highlights the importance of embracing differences, resilience, and empathy, all of which are key elements of a growth mindset.

The Theory of Everything
The life of physicist Stephen Hawking and his unwavering will in the face of ALS (Amyotrophic lateral sclerosis). The movie can serve as a powerful example of perseverance and the capacity to adapt and excel even when life takes an unexpected turn.

Inside Out
A Disney/Pixar film that cleverly illustrates the workings of our emotions and mindset.

Documentaries
Jiro Dreams of Sushi
This documentary follows 85-year-old sushi master Jiro Ono, providing a beautiful and detailed portrayal of mastery and a lifelong pursuit of excellence.

He Named Me Malala
An intimate portrait of Malala Yousafzai, who was targeted by the Taliban and severely wounded by a gunshot when returning home on her school bus in Pakistan's Swat Valley. Her focused pursuit of education and advocacy for girls' education globally despite the odds shows the embodiment of a growth mindset.

In Search of Greatness
This documentary explores the importance of creativity, passion, and mindset in achieving greatness through interviews with various successful athletes.

Free Solo
This documentary follows Alex Honnold as he becomes the first person to ever free solo climb Yosemite's 3,000 foot high El Capitan Wall. With no ropes or safety gear, his determination, preparation, and unwavering belief in himself are potent illustrations of a growth mindset.

A Mindful Choice
A documentary that shows the powerful positive impact of mindfulness meditation

The Social Dilemma
This documentary can spark discussion about the impact of social media on our mindsets.

Podcasts

The Growth Mindset Podcast
This podcast delves into stories of personal change and growth, showcasing how a change in mindset can yield impressive results, relevant to anyone seeking to understand and cultivate a growth mindset.

Freakonomics Radio: How to Make Your Own Luck
This episode explores how luck isn't purely random but can be influenced by our actions and attitudes, a key concept for cultivating a proactive growth mindset.

The Love, Happiness and Success Podcast by Dr. Lisa Marie Bobby
Dr. Bobby provides actionable advice on personal growth, emotional health, and relationships, essential areas in cultivating a well-rounded growth mindset.

The Life Coach School Podcast: Episode 158—Future Self
This episode teaches listeners to visualize and work towards their future selves, promoting long-term thinking and self-improvement, key aspects of a growth mindset.

Where Should We Begin? with Esther Perel
This podcast offers insight into the dynamics of human relationships, an important aspect of personal development and communication in a growth mindset.

Finding Mastery: Conversations with Michael Gervais
Gervais interviews high achievers and explores their mindsets, providing listeners with real-world examples of the growth mindset in action.

The School of Greatness: Mindset and Personal Development
This podcast explores the journeys and mindsets of successful people from various fields, demonstrating the practical application of a growth mindset.

The Mindset Mentor
Hosted by Rob Dial, this podcast provides motivational advice, techniques for developing a positive mindset, and inspirational stories.

The Science of Success
Host Matt Bodnar explores the evidence-based growth mindset, sharing

insights from a variety of fields including psychology, neuroscience, and behavioral science.

The Happiness Lab
Dr. Laurie Santos reveals science-backed strategies to increase happiness and cultivate a more positive outlook on life.

The Tony Robbins Podcast
While not exclusively about mindset, many episodes dive into the concepts of personal development, overcoming challenges, and cultivating resilience.

The Learning Scientists Podcast
This podcast is centered on effective learning strategies and the science behind how we learn, a great resource for students and parents alike.

Other useful articles, blogs, and websites

Stanford's PERTS Mindset Kit
A free online resource for educators and parents to learn about growth mindset and how to implement it.

What Having a "Growth Mindset" Actually Means (Harvard Business Review)
This article from the Harvard Business Review explains the meaning of a growth mindset and how to cultivate it.

Developing a Growth Mindset in Teachers and Staff
An article from Edutopia that can help educators, and by extension, parents, understand how to cultivate a growth mindset.

Teaching Your Child to Have a Growth Mindset
This article from Verywell Family provides practical tips for teaching the growth mindset to teenagers.

Mindset Works: Student Motivation through a Growth Mindset
This website contains research and insights into how a growth mindset can improve student motivation and academic success.

'Growth Mindset' Linked to Higher Test Scores, Student Well-Being in Global Study
Statistics from a study conducted by the Program for International Student Assessment show the disparity of mindsets across students in different countries and how it affects their academic outcomes.

About RaiseYouthRight

Our mission is to give every family the resources, skills, and knowledge to help kids reach their full potential.

Let's face it, teens still face many of the same challenges we did growing up. But now, social media, modern technology, and online schooling add so many new layers of complexity.

A plethora of new challenges. Challenges previous generations never had to deal with...

And that's where we come in.

Our research-backed books, newsletters, and content provide clear practical advice to help you and your teens and tweens master these modern challenges with confidence.

We bring together the expertise of educators, psychologists, and writers, channeling our passion into everything we create.

What's unique about us? Our approach balances fun with depth. While the material is engaging, it also addresses complex and sensitive topics with the seriousness they deserve.

We use simple language that teens can relate to - no boring lectures or textbooks here! Just, practical skills taught in a visual, entertaining, and easy-to-understand way.

Join us on this journey. Together, we'll laugh, learn, and give our youth the skills they need to thrive today and lead tomorrow!

https://raiseyouthright.com
https://twitter.com/raiseyouthright
https://www.Facebook.com/raiseyouthright
https://raiseyouthright.com

Also by RaiseYouthRight

The Essential Money Skills Handbook for Teens

Empower your teen to take control of their financial future with *The Essential Money Skills Handbook for Teens*. If you worry about your teen's money management skills or habits, this handbook is the comprehensive solution you've been seeking. Crafted by an author who believes in the power of financial literacy from a young age, this book demystifies the world of finance for your teen in a fun and engaging way.

This handbook isn't just about acquiring skills, it's about building a financially confident individual who can navigate the world of money with ease. From learning to spot financial frauds to understanding why and how to donate, we cover it all. Plus, we've included practical strategies and templates that your teen can start using immediately.

Don't let your teen enter adulthood unprepared for the financial challenges that lie ahead. Grab *The Essential Money Skills Handbook for Teens* today, and watch them embark on a journey that not only assures their financial independence, but also instills a sense of freedom, control, and peace of mind. Your teen deserves a secure financial future—and the journey starts now.

The Essential Social Skills Handbook for Teens

Unlock your teen's full potential with The *Essential Social Skills Handbook for Teens.* If your teen struggles with anxiety, lack of confidence, or shyness, this book is the transformative solution you've been searching for. Written by an author who has personally overcome these challenges, this handbook offers practical techniques and valuable insights to boost your teen's confidence in just 30 days. Say goodbye to social anxieties and hello to a new level of self-assurance. From effective communication strategies to mastering social interactions, this book covers it all. With proven methods and bonus templates, your teen will develop the skills needed to thrive in social situations, set goals, and unleash their true potential. Don't let your teen miss out on the opportunity to become the socially confident individual they deserve to be.

The Essential Career Planning Handbook for Teens

Discover the ultimate career planning guide designed specifically for teens in the modern era. In *The Essential Career Planning Handbook for Teens*, unlock the keys to crafting a path towards a fulfilling and successful future. Packed with expert guidance, actionable strategies, and empowering advice, this book equips both teens and parents with the tools they need to navigate the complex world of career choices and opportunities. From unleashing their unique strengths to mastering the art of networking, teens will gain invaluable insights to propel their career journey forward. Don't leave their future to chance—grab your copy today and embark on an adventure that will shape their path for years to come. The journey to a thriving career starts now!

The Essential Stress Management Handbook for Teens

Discover the ultimate stress management guide designed specifically for teens in the post-pandemic era. In *The Essential Stress Management Handbook for Teens*, you'll unlock the keys to conquering stress and empowering your teens to thrive. With practical strategies, proven techniques, and personalized advice, this book equips both teens and parents with the tools they need to navigate the pressures of school, digital overload, and social challenges. From agile stress-relief techniques to habit-forming exercises, you'll learn how to transform stress-busting hacks into natural instincts that empower your teens to tackle stress head-on. Don't let stress hinder your teens' happiness and success—grab your copy today and embark on a journey toward a stress-free and fulfilling life.

Made in the USA
Coppell, TX
12 December 2024

42377344R00089